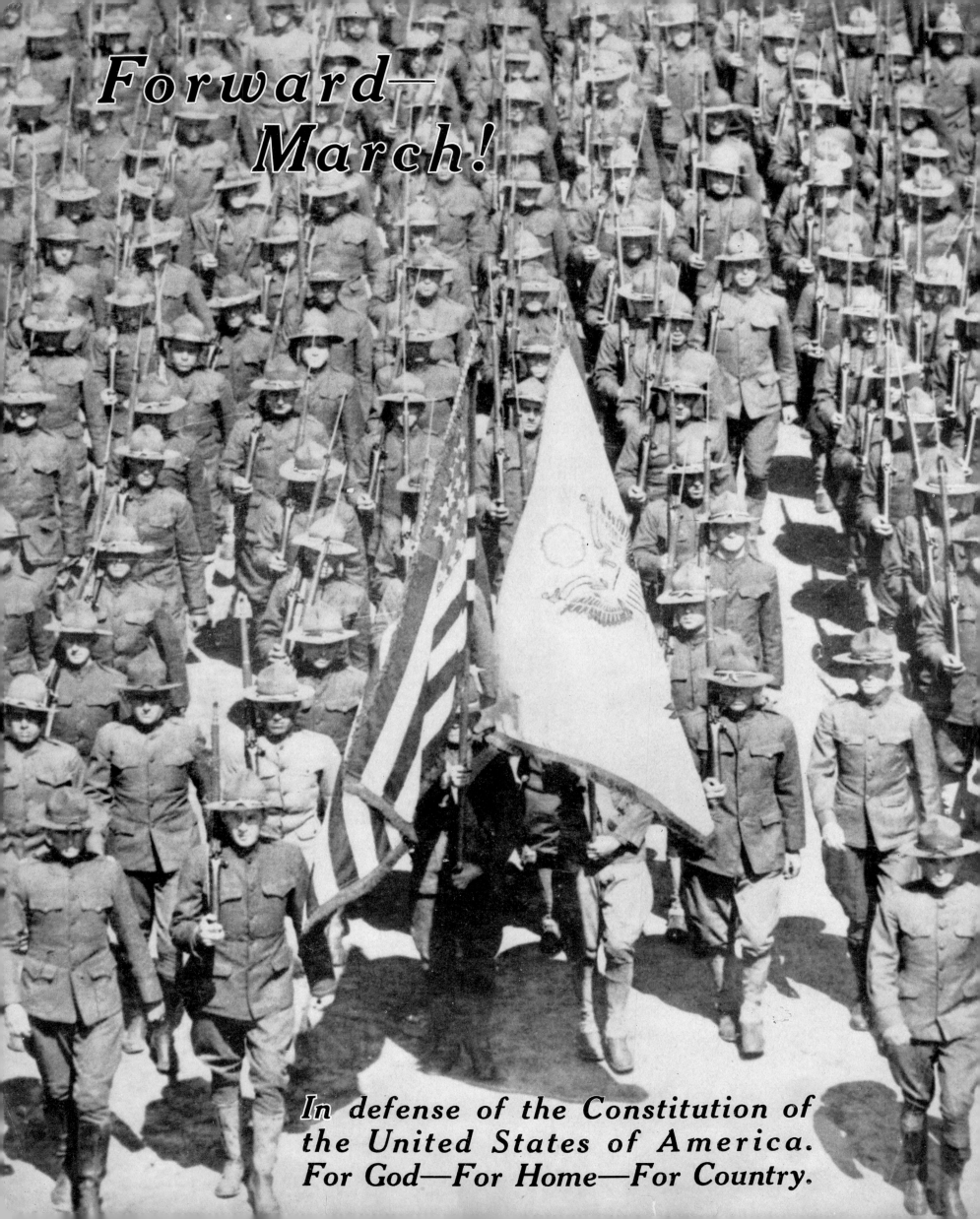

Forward—
March!

In defense of the Constitution of
the United States of America.
For God—For Home—For Country.

FORWARD-MARCH!

SECTION ONE

THE PHOTOGRAPHIC RECORD OF
AMERICA IN THE WORLD WAR AND
THE POST WAR SOCIAL UPHEAVAL

By

FRANK J. MACKEY

and

MARCUS WILSON JERNEGAN, Ph. D.

Advisory Editor

THE DISABLED AMERICAN VETERANS OF THE WORLD WAR

DEPARTMENT OF REHABILITATION

CHICAGO

┌───┐

~ DEDICATED ~

—to the soldier-camera men, known and unknown
—to those who lived to develop their negatives and
—to those who made the supreme sacrifice,
—that posterity might see and might know.

└───┘

ACKNOWLEDGMENTS

We gratefully acknowledge the courtesy of the Department of War for permission to use on the outside cover of Forward-March!, a replica of The Distinguished Service Cross. The cooperation of the various U. S. official photo divisions, private collectors and news gathering agencies is deeply appreciated. The right to reproduce any photograph is reserved by the individual copyright owner, from whom rights for publication in Forward-March! were acquired. No part of Forward-March! may be reproduced in any form or used for advertising, solicitation or promotion purposes without the written permission of the Disabled American Veterans of the World War, Department of Rehabilitation.

ROBERT LINDNEUX
GENERAL CHARLES G. DAWES
U. S. SIGNAL CORPS OFFICIAL PHOTOS
U. S. NAVY OFFICIAL PHOTOS
HQ. 6TH CORPS AREA
AMERICAN BATTLE MONUMENTS COMMISSION
HENRY MILLER, NEWS PICTURE SERVICE
ACME NEWSPICTURES, INC.
UNDERWOOD & UNDERWOOD
INTERNATIONAL NEWS
OTTO KURTH

WIDE WORLD
TIMES PHOTOS
BROWN & BIGELOW
CARL W. RAWSON
CURTIS & CAMERON
EWING GALLOWAY
HARRIS EWING
UNIVERSAL PICTURES
KEYSTONE VIEW CO.
ASSOCIATED PRESS
PACIFIC AND ATLANTIC PHOTOS

Introduction

We shall fight for the things we have always carried nearest our hearts—for democracy—for the right of those who submit to authority to have a voice in their government.

These immortal words spoken by Woodrow Wilson on April 2, 1917, sent us into war. For eighteen months every activity of the nation was directed towards the single goal—Victory. Four million men offered their bodies. Other millions offered their time, their energies, and their fortunes for the one purpose. Mothers gave their sons, children gave their fathers, "that government of the people, by the people, and for the people shall not perish from the earth."

The passing years have blurred the outline of memory for many who took part in these stirring scenes. To all such "Forward-March!" will be a welcome memento. For those who were unable to take an active part and to those who were as yet unborn or too young to realize what was happening, this photographic record will bring a clear perception, an undistorted understanding of the World War and its aftermath.

The detail and composition of many of these pictures represent the height of achievement in the art of photography. Most troop movements were at night—the infantry usually jumped off at the first appearance of dawn—and it really did rain in France. Therefore, it is not surprising that a few of the photographs are totally lacking in the qualities that go to make a good picture. With shells exploding and bullets whistling, the photographers did not always pause to adjust the focus or time the exposure.

If it be true that, "one picture is worth a hundred printed pages," this work will fill a long felt need in the field of historical information. It is our purpose to show faithfully, the war as we knew it—the horror and tragedy, the sublime heights of courage, and even the comedy and pathos, that were all a part of "the great adventure." Every fine distinction has been observed in the selections. Photographs which might further distress Gold Star mothers have, in so far as possible, been omitted. It is not necessary to deliberately select gruesome pictures in order to prove that Sherman was right.

We are now far enough removed from the conflict to get a clear perspective. We know that the World War began long before 1914—we are not sure that it is now ended. The scenes depicted here are but the genesis of the events we are living today. Lost souls, broken bodies, foundered institutions, Communism, Fascism, Naziism and other isms yet to come, are the natural aftermath of this trial by the sword.

In no sense can "Forward-March!" be interpreted as propaganda. We simply state the facts—all of the facts. The World War definitely marks the beginning of a new epoch. Every essential event beginning with the period of neutrality, up through the tidal wave of social unrest, that has followed in the wake of the world clash of arms, is covered in detail. The majority of the photographs are U. S. Official. Many of them have never before been released. Most of them

are identified—time, place and outfit. Some, developed from negatives from cameras picked up out in No Man's Land, probably never will be identified. The soldier-camera man who made the exposures, also made the supreme sacrifice, that posterity might see and might know. The captions tell the authentic story. Documents from the government archives here reproduced are, we believe, all important in the study of the past two decades of mankind's struggle. The statistical information is as accurate as governmental research can make it.

The purpose of the publication of "Forward-March!" is threefold:

To form a background of understanding for the social, political and economic trends of today and tomorrow.

To preserve intact, in picture and story, the important events of the greatest cataclysm in the history of man, that present and future generations, who have not been through the furnace of armed conflict might learn, through the all-seeing camera eye, just how much "glory and romance" there really is in war.

Believing in evolution of government rather than revolution, we feel that the facts contained in these portfolios will be instrumental in combating the subversive doctrines of Communism and other insidious foreign propaganda, designed to overthrow by force the free democracy which took root and flourished on American soil. Our comrades fought and died in defense of that democracy.

In conceiving "Forward-March!", we have been ever conscious of these lines penned by Col. John McCrae:

"Take up our quarrel with the foe!
To you from failing hands we throw
The Torch—be yours to hold it high;
If ye break faith with us who die,
We shall not sleep, though poppies grow
In Flanders' fields."

The foe was not the German people. America had no quarrel with them. The foe was, and still is, Autocracy. It is only right that they who bear the visible and invisible scars of the conflict against the enemy receive and accept The Torch. We shall strive to "hold it high" and carry on—not with the sword, but with education.

Attention!

Forward-MARCH!

DISABLED AMERICAN VETERANS OF THE WORLD WAR

Volney F. Mooney Jr.

National Commander

Attest: *Vivian D. Corbly*

National Adjutant

Arrangement of Forward-March! Portfolios

SECTION ONE

SECTION TWO

AS MILLIONS CHEERED

"NOTHING WILL BE TOO GOOD FOR YOU WHEN YOU RETURN," SHOUTED THE MILLIONS.
FAMILIAR SCENES IN EVERY AMERICAN CITY WHEN THE BOYS LEFT FOR OVER-SEAS.
NEW YORK (Upper Left) CHICAGO (Upper Right) BOSTON (Lower Left)

America Learns That War Can "Touch Us"

When the "European War" broke out in 1914 Americans, on the whole, took the attitude that it was none of our business and that nothing could induce us to go into it. "It can't touch us" seemed to be the principal editorial and oratorical theme. America forgot, or failed in, the lessons she should have learned during the Napoleonic Wars. We know now, after a bitter experience, that we are involved in the policies of Europe and that keeping out of a general European conflagration will always be extremely difficult, if not impossible.

At the outbreak of the War there was very little deep pro-Ally or pro-German sentiment in the United States; in fact, the country was strongly pro-American. As the War progressed, American citizens began allying themselves into groups known as German-Americans, Polish-Americans and what not. On the high seas there was constant interference with American commerce by the Allies, the principal offender being England, and by Germany. Great Britain claimed that ships bound for Norway, Sweden, Denmark, and Holland were subject to seizure. American ships bound for these neutral countries were seized by Great Britain and taken to a British port to be leisurely searched for what the Allies listed as contraband, which now included food and practically everything useful. While these acts aroused much resentment against England, the torpedoing of ships by Germany tended toward the crystallization of Allied sympathy. Numerous ships sunk without warning, caused the loss of American life. These incidents were followed by lengthy correspondence between the two governments, always culminating with expressions of regret and promises of indemnity on the part of the Imperial German Government.

On April 30, 1915, the advertisements of the Cunard Line sailings had immediately beneath them the following extraordinary notice:

NOTICE.—Travelers intending to embark on the Atlantic voyage are reminded that a state of war exists between Germany and her allies and Great Britain and her allies; that the zone of war includes the water adjacent to the British Isles; that in accordance with formal notice given by the Imperial German Government, vessels flying the flag of Great Britain or any of her allies are liable to destruction in these waters and that travelers sailing in the war zone on ships of Great Britain or her allies do so at their own risk. IMPERIAL GERMAN EMBASSY

Washington, D. C., April 22, 1915.

The notice was not taken seriously as no one believed that any government could think of doing what the notice implied. On May 7, 1915, the Lusitania, eight miles off the southern coast of Ireland, had two torpedoes split into her sides, without warning. Of the 1,924 passengers, 35 of whom were babies, 1,198—including all but 4 of the babies—were drowned. Of the 188 Americans aboard, 114 were drowned. America stood appalled. The demands for a declaration of war against Germany came from the press and the public.

On July 24, 1915, Doctor Heinrich E. Albert, German Councilor, lost his brief case on a New York elevated train. It was picked up by Frank Burke, an operative of the U. S. Secret Service Department, who had been shadowing the German. The papers in Herr Doktor's brief case were marked "Streng Vertraulich" but Burke did not know that this meant "strictly confidential." The contents revealed that under Dr. Albert's direction:

The German Government had spent twenty-eight million dollars on propaganda and plots in the United States;

German spies had placed time fire bombs on steamships departing from the United States;

A German spy had been given money and had been sent to Buffalo to blow up the Welland Canal;

Spies had been sent to foment strikes and start fires in American industrial plants;

Two million dollars had been spent on coal which was ostensibly shipped to South America, but was delivered to German raiders;

Germany's agents had forged passports to enable German spies to enter America, and to enter Allied countries through America.

The publication of the information from this "Pandora's Box" tended to swing sentiment definitely against Germany. The United States immediately demanded that Germany recall its military and naval attachés from this embassy, Captain Franz von Papen and Captain Karl von Boy-Ed, and that Austria recall its ambassador, Doctor Constantine Dumba. The war clouds were gathering.

Only the steadying influence of Woodrow Wilson kept us out of the war at this time. Correspondence between the two governments on the Lusitania affair continued for nearly a year during which time submarine warfare continued. On April 18, 1916, Woodrow Wilson addressed his final note to Germany:

"[The] roll of Americans who have lost their lives upon ships thus attacked . . . . has grown month by month until the ominous toll has mounted into the hundreds. [The United States had] been willing to wait until the facts became unmistakable and were susceptible of only one interpretation . . . . It now owes it to a just regard for its own rights to say to the Imperial German Government that that time has come . . . . Unless the Imperial German Government should now immediately declare and effect an abandonment of its present methods of submarine warfare, the government of the United States can have no other choice but to sever diplomatic relations with the German Empire."

To this ultimatum Germany replied on May 4, 1916, advising that the German Naval forces had been given the following orders:

Merchant vessels . . . . shall not be sunk without warning and without saving human lives unless those ships attempt to escape or offer resistance.

Woodrow Wilson won his point but during the long negotiations the American Press had hurled unkind epithets at him for using words instead of bullets. That the majority of Americans were in sympathy with the President's course is evidenced by the fact that he was re-elected, though by a narrow margin, in 1916, on the slogan: "He kept us out of war."

For nine months German submarine warfare was restricted to the Wilson limits. However, Great Britain continued to seize all American ships bound for neutral countries bordering Germany. Over eighty American firms were "black listed" by Great Britain on the suspicion that they were trading with Germany indirectly, which was their right, if they could. This prevented their trading with neutrals. Without British approval an American firm could not do business with Europe. Before "permission" was granted to any firm it had to furnish the British Embassy with a list of its customers. These lists then became available to British competitors. Britain rifled American mails and filched American trade secrets. International law was ignored and violated every day by Britain. Only the diplomacy of Walter Hines Page, American Ambassador to the court of St. James, was delaying the break of diplomatic relations with Britain. Anti-British sentiment in America was growing strong and the President was discussing the advisability of notifying England that American merchantmen would be sent with convoys, when Germany made its prize blunder.

On January 31, 1917, Count Johann von Bernstorff, the German Ambassador, handed to the American Government a note announcing that on February 1, Germany would begin unrestricted warfare and would "forcibly prevent" any vessel of the United States (or of any country) from going to England, except that it would permit the United States to send one passenger vessel each week, provided: It must go to the Port of Falmouth; it must arrive on a Sunday; it must leave on a Wednesday; it must travel by a specified course; it must be marked in a special way; the United States must guarantee that the ship carry nothing on the German contraband list.

The American people were utterly shocked. The grievances against England were forgotten. The demand for severance of diplomatic relations with Germany became almost universal. It was felt that no greater insult had been offered to any people; that to submit to Germany would prevent our ever again posing as a nation of free people; that if we submitted, Japan or any other country could, at any time in the future, issue similar or even more humiliating orders.

On February 3, 1917, President Wilson, in an address to Congress, said: "I think you will agree with me that this government has no alternative consistent with the dignity and honor of the United States; . . . I have, therefore, directed the Secretary of State to announce to his Excellency, the German Ambassador, that all diplomatic relations between the United States and the German Empire are severed, and to hand to his Excellency his passports."

On February 24, 1917, Walter Hines Page, the American Ambassador to England, advised his government that the following message from the German Government to the German Minister to Mexico had been intercepted:

"We intend to begin on the first of February unrestricted submarine warfare. We shall endeavor in spite of this to keep the United States of America neutral. In the event of this not succeeding, we make Mexico a proposal of alliance on the following basis: make war together, make peace together, generous financial support and an understanding on our part that Mexico is to reconquer her lost territory in Texas, New Mexico, and Arizona. The settlement in detail is left to you. You will inform the President (President Carranza of Mexico) of the above most secretly as soon as the outbreak of war with the United States of America is certain."

Alfred Zimmermann, the German Minister of Foreign Affairs, frankly admitted the authorship of the note, but emphasized that "the instructions were only to be carried out after declaration of war by America."

The House of Representatives immediately passed, by a vote of 403 to 13, a bill authorizing the President to arm merchant ships. In the Senate, 11 Senators, led by LaFollette of Wisconsin, filibustered for three days until the "Lame Duck" session ended on March 4 and prevented the other 75 Senators from voting on the bill.

However, the Attorney-General advised the President that without specific authorization by Congress he had the power to place gunners on merchant ships as protection against the submarines. On March 9, the President announced that this would be done, and at the same time issued a call for a special session of Congress, to meet on April 16.

Germany's reply to the President's order was a proclamation announcing that American gunners would be taken from the American merchant ships and executed as pirates. The proclamation was so unreasonable that the President advanced the call for the special session to April 2, "to receive a communication concerning grave matters."

Within a week three American vessels, the Illinois, the Vigilancia and the City of Memphis, were torpedoed and sunk without warning. On the afternoon of April 2, 1917, the President delivered his immortal war speech, asking that the United States accept the status of belligerent which had been thrust upon her by Germany. On Good Friday, April 6, the declaration of war was passed by the House of Representatives by a vote of 373 to 50, and in the Senate by a vote of 82 to 6. The bill was immediately signed by the President.

MOBILIZING THE AMERICAN MIND

Notwithstanding the fact that the declaration of war with Germany met with the approval of the great majority of the American people, who preferred war to national humiliation, it was thought necessary to create "The Committee on Public Information." The principal purpose of this committee was to mobilize the American mind and make America war-conscious.

Under the able leadership of George Creel, every avenue of publicity and every possible attention-compelling device were used. The artists, cartoonists, and illustrators were mobilized to prepare posters, which covered barns, billboards, and street corners. The advertising men, novelists, dramatists, moving picture producers, and college professors were mobilized to do their bit in their respective fields. The "Four Minute Men", 75,000 strong, were selected from volunteers who at theaters, lodge meetings, labor meetings, schools, churches, or wherever citizens gathered, delivered four minute speeches prepared under George Creel's direction. A total of 314,454,514 groups were contacted.

The first subject discussed was: "Universal Service by Selective Draft." This was for the purpose of preventing a repetition of the draft riots of Civil War days. When Liberty Bond drives were on, the Four Minute Men urged the public to invest. Among other subjects discussed were "Food Conservation," "Support the Red Cross," "Why We Are Fighting," "Maintaining Morals and Morale," "The Importance of Speed," and, to offset German propaganda, "Where Did You Get Your Facts?"

The Committee on Public Information also gave out the news to Washington correspondents. Creel had no censorship on war news except as the newspapers would impose on themselves, after he had explained the necessity. News, good or bad, was not suppressed. There were no exaggerated claims of victories won. Losses were not minimized. This was quite different from the strict censorship and false statements released by all of the other belligerents.

The net cost to the taxpayers for this propaganda committee was $4,912,553. George Creel reached his objective. As an organizer he was a genius. Through his efforts the American mind was mobilized, America was made war-conscious, minorities were silenced, and the government was enthusiastically supported.

CENTRALIZATION OF POWER

The Magna Carta was signed in June, 1215. Practically all political changes, from that day up to the World War, had been in taking power away from the state, for the benefit of the individual. Six months after our entry into the war, the individual had been, through the use of propaganda, clever slogans, and pep talks, induced to surrender the liberties, which centuries of contest had given him.

Every man between 18 and 45 was asked to surrender his body; 163,738 were arrested and many sent to jail for refusing.

No one was permitted to talk against the method or purpose of the war; 1597 were arrested for violation.

The use of gold and silver for artistic or industrial purposes was prohibited.

Factories engaged in war work could not advertise for unskilled labor.

Tire manufacturers were ordered to cut production 50 per cent by August 1, 1918.

After February 15, 1918, no imports or exports were permitted except by special license.

Bakery products must contain 20 per cent wheat substitutes.

Clocks had to be advanced one hour, (Daylight Savings Time).

Sugar rations, three pounds per month per person; reduced to two pounds on July 26, 1918.

The meat packing industry was put under Federal license June 18, 1918.

The entire wheat crop was taken over by the government at $2.20 per bushel (May 15, 1918).

Use of coal or fuel oil was prohibited on pleasure yachts.

The Federal Fuel Administrator ordered 170 silk factories in Patterson, N. J., closed (January 3, 1918).

The government took over and operated the railroads, express companies, telephone, telegraph and coal mines.

Automobile manufacturers were ordered to cut production 25 per cent (June 10, 1918) and to convert their plants to 100 per cent war work by January 1, 1919.

Lightless nights and meatless days were ordered. People were requested not to drive automobiles, motorcycles, or motorboats on Sundays; the few who disregarded this request were roughly treated by enraged citizens. Factories not engaged in war work were ordered closed in various sections of the country at various times.

The American people willingly gave up their liberty, assuming that the passing of the emergency meant its restoration. However, the records show that governments have learned that by the use of clever slogans and the declaration that an emergency exists, it is possible for the National mind to be mobilized. Since the World War the tendency has been to give to the central government many of the rights which during recent centuries have been regarded as belonging entirely to the individual.

Gen. Paul von Hindenburg, Chief of General Staff with
Erich Ludendorff, Quartermaster General, German Armies.

Kaiser William II. and his six warrior sons
on parade in Berlin.

American steamship sinking.   Neptune takes his toll.   A direct hit.

The Declaration of Americanism

By WOODROW WILSON

Personally Delivered to the Senate and House of Representatives
Assembled in Extraordinary Session
April Second, Nineteen Hundred and Seventeen

GENTLEMEN OF THE CONGRESS:

I have called the Congress into extraordinary session because there are serious, very serious, choices of policy to be made, and made immediately, which it was neither right nor constitutionally permissible that I should assume the responsibility of making.

On the third of February last I officially laid before you the extraordinary announcement of the Imperial German Government that on and after the first day of February it was its purpose to put aside all restraints of law or of humanity and use its submarines to sink every vessel that sought to approach either the ports of Great Britain and Ireland or the western coasts of Europe or any of the ports controlled by the enemies of Germany within the Mediterranean. That had seemed to be the object of the German submarine warfare earlier in the war, but since April of last year the Imperial Government had somewhat restrained the commanders of its undersea craft in conformity with its promise then given to us that passenger boats should not be sunk and that due warning would be given to all other vessels which its submarines might seek to destroy, when no resistance was offered or escape attempted, and care taken that their crews were given at least a fair chance to save their lives in their open boats. The precautions taken were meager and haphazard enough, as was proved in distressing instance after instance in the progress of the cruel and unmanly business, but a certain degree of restraint was observed. The new policy has swept every restriction aside. Vessels of every kind, whatever their flag, their character, their cargo, their destination, their errand, have been ruthlessly sent to the bottom without warning and without thought of help or mercy for those on board, the vessels of friendly neutrals along with those of belligerents. Even hospital ships and ships carrying relief to the sorely bereaved and stricken people of Belgium, though the latter were provided with safe conduct through the proscribed areas by the German Government itself and were distinguished by unmistakable marks of identity, have been sunk with the same reckless lack of compassion or of principle.

I was for a little while unable to believe that such things would in fact be done by any government that had hitherto subscribed to the humane practices of civilized nations. International law had its origin in the attempt to set up some law which would be respected and observed upon the seas, where no nation had right of dominion and where lay the free highways of the world. By painful stage after stage has that law been built up, with meager enough results, indeed, after all was accomplished that could be accomplished, but always with a clear view, at least, of what the heart and conscience of mankind demanded. This minimum of right the German Government has swept aside under the plea of retaliation and necessity and because it had no weapons which it could use at sea except these which it is impossible to employ as it is employing them without throwing to the

THE WAR PRESIDENT

winds all scruples of humanity or of respect for the understandings that were supposed to underlie the intercourse of the world. I am not now thinking of the loss of property involved, immense and serious as that is, but only of the wanton and wholesale destruction of the lives of non-combatants, men, women, and children, engaged in pursuits which have always, even in the darkest periods of modern history, been deemed innocent and legitimate. Property can be paid for; the lives of peaceful and innocent people cannot be. The present German submarine warfare against commerce is a warfare against mankind.

"A prophet is not without honor, save in his own country and in his own house." Unfortunately, American statesmen do not receive due recognition until their political generation has passed. This was true of Washington, of Lincoln, and of all others. Some day this address will undoubtedly be recognized as one of the outstanding documents in America's archives. The diction is superb. The argument and appeal are unsurpassed.

It is a war against all nations. American ships have been sunk, American lives taken, in ways which it has stirred us very deeply to learn of, but the ships and people of other neutral and friendly nations have been sunk and overwhelmed in the waters in the same way. There has been no discrimination. The challenge is to all mankind. Each nation must decide for itself how it will meet it. The choice we make for ourselves must be made with a moderation of counsel and a temperateness of judgment befitting our character and our motives as a nation. We must put excited feeling away. Our motive will not be revenge or the victorious assertion of the physical might of the nation, but only the vindication of right, of human right, of which we are only a single champion.

When I addressed the Congress on the twenty-sixth of February last I thought that it would suffice to assert our neutral rights with arms, our right to use the seas against unlawful interference, our right to keep our people safe against unlawful violence. But armed neutrality, it now appears, is impracticable. Because submarines are in effect outlaws when used as the German submarines have been used against merchant shipping, it is impossible to defend ships against their attacks as the law of nations has assumed that merchantmen would defend themselves against privateers or cruisers, visible craft giving chase upon the open sea. It is common prudence in such circumstances, grim necessity indeed, to endeavor to destroy them before they have shown their own intention. They must be dealt with upon sight, if dealt with at all. The German Government denies the right of neutrals to use arms at all within the areas of the sea which it has proscribed, even in the defense of rights which no modern publicist has ever before questioned their right to defend. The intimation is conveyed that the armed guards which we have placed on our merchant ships will be treated as beyond the pale of law and subject to be dealt with as pirates would be. Armed neutrality is ineffectual enough at best; in such circumstances and in the face of such pretensions it is worse than ineffectual; it is likely only to produce what it was meant to prevent; it is practically certain to draw us into the war without either the rights or the effectiveness of belligerents. There is one choice we cannot make, we are incapable of making: we will not choose the path of submission and suffer the most sacred rights of our nation and our people to be ignored or violated. The wrongs against which we now array ourselves are no common wrongs; they cut to the very roots of human life.

With a profound sense of the solemn and even tragical character of the step I am taking and of the grave responsibilities which it involves, but in unhesitating obedience to what I deem my constitutional duty, I advise that the Congress declare the recent course of the Imperial German Government to be in fact nothing less than war against the government and people of the United States: that it formally accept the status of belligerent which has thus been thrust upon it; and that it take immediate steps not only to put the country in a more thorough state of defense but also to exert all its power and employ all its resources to bring the Government of the German Empire to terms and end the war.

What this will involve is clear. It will involve the utmost practicable co-operation in counsel and action with the governments now at war with Germany, and, as incident to that, the extension to those governments of the most liberal financial credits, in order that our resources may so far as possible be added to theirs. It will involve the organization and mobilization of all the material resources of the country to supply the materials of war and serve the incidental needs of the nation in the most abundant and yet the most economical and efficient way possible. It will involve the immediate full equipment of the navy in all respects, but particularly in supplying it with the best means of dealing with the enemy's submarines. It will involve the immediate addition to the armed forces of the United States already provided for by law in case of war at least five hundred thousand men, who should, in my opinion, be chosen upon the principle of universal liability to service, and also the authorization of subsequent additional increments of equal force so soon as they may be needed and can be handled in training. It will involve also, of course, the granting of adequate credits to the Government, sustained, I hope, so far as they can equitably be sustained by the present generation, by well conceived taxation.

I say sustained so far as may be equitable by taxation because it seems to me that it would be most unwise to base the credits which will now be necessary entirely on money borrowed. It is our duty, I most respectfully urge, to protect our people so far as we may against

the very serious hardships and evils which would be likely to arise out of the inflation which would be produced by vast loans.

In carrying out the measures by which these things are to be accomplished we should keep constantly in mind the wisdom of interfering as little as possible in our own preparation and in the equipment of our own military forces with the duty,—for it will be a very practical duty,—of supplying the nations already at war with Germany with the materials which they can obtain only from us or by our assistance.

They are in the field and we should help them in every way to be effective there.

I shall take the liberty of suggesting, through the several executive departments of the Government, for the consideration of your committees, measures for the accomplishment of the several objects I have mentioned. I hope that it will be your pleasure to deal with them as having been framed after very careful thought by the branch of the Government upon which the responsibility of conducting the war and safeguarding the nation will most directly fall.

While we do these things, these deeply momentous things, let us be very clear, and make very clear to all the world what our motives and our objects are. My own thought has not been driven from its habitual and normal course by the unhappy events of the last two months, and I do not believe that the thought of the nation has been altered or clouded by them. I have exactly the same things in mind now that I had in mind when I addressed the Senate on the twenty-second of January last; the same that I had in mind when I addressed the Congress on the third of February and on the twenty-sixth of February. Our object now, as then, is to vindicate the principles of peace and justice in the life of the world as against selfish and autocratic power and to set up amongst the really free and self-governed peoples of the world such a concert of purpose and of action as will henceforth ensure the observance of those principles. Neutrality is no longer feasible or desirable where the peace of the world is involved and the freedom of its peoples, and the menace to that peace and freedom lies in the existence of autocratic governments backed by organized force which is controlled wholly by their will, not by the will of their people. We have seen the last of neutrality in such circumstances. We are at the beginning of an age in which it will be insisted that the same standards of conduct and of responsibility for wrong done shall be observed among nations and their governments that are observed among the individual citizens of civilized states.

We have no quarrel with the German people. We have no feeling towards them but one of sympathy and friendship. It was not upon their impulse that their government acted in entering this war. It was not with their previous knowledge or approval. It was a war determined upon as wars used to be determined upon in the old, unhappy days when peoples were nowhere consulted by their rulers and wars were provoked and waged in the interest of dynasties or of little groups of ambitious men who were accustomed to use their fellowmen as pawns and tools.

Self-governed nations do not fill their neighbor states with spies or set the course of intrigue to bring about some critical posture of affairs which will give them an opportunity to strike and make conquest. Such designs can be successfully worked out only under cover and where no one has the right to ask questions. Cunningly contrived plans of deception or aggression, carried, it may be, from generation to generation, can be worked out and kept from the light only within the privacy of courts or behind the carefully guarded confidences of a narrow and privileged class. They are happily impossible where public opinion commands and insists upon full information concerning all the nation's affairs.

A steadfast concert for peace can never be maintained except by a partnership of democratic nations. No autocratic government could be trusted to keep faith within it or observe its covenants. It must be a league of honor, a partnership of opinion. Intrigue would eat its vitals away; the plottings of inner circles who could plan what they would and render account to no one would be a corruption seated at its very heart. Only free peoples can hold their purpose and their honor steady to a common end and prefer the interests of mankind to any narrow interest of their own.

One of the things that has served to convince us that the Prussian autocracy was not and could never be our friend is that from the very outset of the present war it has filled our unsuspecting communities and even our offices of government with spies and set criminal intrigues everywhere afoot against our national unity of counsel, our peace within and without, our industries and our commerce. Indeed it is now evident that its spies were here even before the war began; and it is unhappily not a matter of conjecture but a fact proved in our courts of justice that the intrigues which have more than once come perilously near to disturbing the peace and dislocating the industries of the country have been carried on at the instigation, with the support, and even under the personal direction of official agents of the Imperial Government accredited to the Government of the United States. Even in checking these things and trying to extirpate them we have sought to put the most generous interpretation possible upon them because we knew that their source lay, not in any hostile feeling or purpose of the German people towards us (who were, no doubt as ignorant of them as we ourselves were), but only in the selfish designs of a Government that did what it pleased and told its people nothing. But they have played their part in serving to convince us at last that that Government entertains no real friendship for us and means to act against our peace and security at its convenience. That it means to stir up enemies against us at our very doors the intercepted note to the German Minister at Mexico City is eloquent evidence.

We are accepting this challenge of hostile purpose because we know that in such a government, following such methods, we can never have a friend; and that in the presence of its organized power, always lying in wait to accomplish we know not what purpose, there can be no assured security for the democratic governments of the world. We are now about to accept gauge of battle with this natural foe to liberty and shall, if necessary, spend the whole force of the nation to check and nullify its pretensions and its power. We are glad, now that we see the facts with no veil of false pretense about them, to fight thus for the ultimate peace of the world and for the liberation of its peoples, the German peoples included: for the rights of nations great and small and the privilege of men everywhere to choose their way of life and of obedience. The world must be made safe for democracy. Its peace must be planted upon the tested foundations of political liberty. We have no selfish ends to serve. We desire no conquest, no dominion. We seek no indemnities for ourselves, no material compensation for the sacrifices we shall freely make. We are but one of the champions of the rights of mankind. We shall be satisfied when those rights have been made as secure as the faith and the freedom of nations can make them.

Just because we fight without rancor and without selfish object, seeking nothing for ourselves but what we shall wish to share with all free peoples, we shall, I feel confident, conduct our operations as belligerents without passion and ourselves observe with proud punctilio the principles of right and of fair play we profess to be fighting for.

I have said nothing of the governments allied with the Imperial Government of Germany because they have not made war upon us or challenged us to defend our right and our honor. The Austro-Hungarian Government has, indeed, avowed its unqualified endorsement and acceptance of the reckless and lawless submarine warfare adopted now without disguise by the Imperial German Government, and it has therefore not been possible for this Government to receive Count Tarnowski, the Ambassador recently accredited to this Government by the Imperial and Royal Government of Austria-Hungary; but

that Government has not actually engaged in warfare against citizens of the United States on the seas, and I take the liberty, for the present at least, of postponing a discussion of our relations with the authorities at Vienna. We enter this war only where we are clearly forced into it because there are no other means of defending our rights.

It will be all the easier for us to conduct ourselves as belligerents in a high spirit of right and fairness because we act without animus, not in enmity towards a people or with the desire to bring any injury or disadvantage upon them, but only in armed opposition to an irresponsible government which has thrown aside all considerations of humanity and of right and is running amuck. We are, let me say again, the sincere friends of the German people, and shall desire nothing so much as the early re-establishment of intimate relations of mutual advantage between us,—however hard it may be for them, for the time being, to believe that this is spoken from our hearts. We have borne with their present government through all these bitter months because of that friendship,—exercising a patience and forbearance which would otherwise have been impossible. We shall, happily, still have an opportunity to prove that friendship in our daily attitude and actions towards the millions of men and women of German birth and native sympathy who live amongst us and share our life, and we shall be proud to prove it towards all who are in fact loyal to their neighbors and to the Government in the hour of test. They are, most of them, as true and loyal Americans as if they had never known any other fealty or allegiance. They will be prompt to stand with us in rebuking and restraining the few who may be of a different mind and purpose. If there should be disloyalty, it will be dealt with with a firm hand of stern repression; but, if it lifts its head at all, it will lift it only here and there and without countenance except from a lawless and malignant few.

It is a distressing and oppressive duty, Gentlemen of the Congress, which I have performed in thus addressing you. There are, it may be, many months of fiery trial and sacrifice ahead of us.

It is a fearful thing to lead this great peaceful people into war, into the most terrible and disastrous of all wars, civilization itself seeming to be in the balance. But the right is more precious than peace, and we shall fight for the things which we have always carried nearest our hearts,—for democracy, for the right of those who submit to authority to have a voice in their own governments, for the rights and liberties of small nations, for a universal dominion of right by such a concert of free peoples as shall bring peace and safety to all nations and make the world itself at last free. To such a task we can dedicate our lives and our fortunes, everything that we are and everything that we have, with the pride of those who know that the day has come when America is privileged to spend her blood and her might for the principles that gave her birth and happiness and the peace which she has treasured.

GOD HELPING HER, SHE CAN DO NO OTHER.

GENERAL JOHN J. PERSHING

From a painting by Robert Lindneux. Reproduced by special courtesy of General Charles G. Dawes, owner of the original.

The Commander-in-Chief
GENERAL JOHN J. PERSHING
Accounts for His Stewardship

General Headquarters American Expeditionary Forces.

To the Secretary of War.   SEPTEMBER 1, 1919.

Sir: I have the honor to submit herewith my final report as Commander-in-Chief of the American Expeditionary Forces in Europe:

1. I assumed the duties of this office on May 26, 1917, and, accompanied by a small staff, departed for Europe on board the S. S. *Baltic* May 28. We arrived at London on June 9 and, after spending some days in consultation with the British authorities, reached Paris on June 13.

2. Following the rather earnest appeals of the Allies for American troops, it was decided to send to France, at once, 1 complete division and 9 newly organized regiments of engineers. The division was formed of regular regiments, necessary transfers of officers and men were made, and recruits were assigned to increase these units to the required strength.

The offer by the Navy Department of one regiment of marines to be reorganized as infantry was accepted by the Secretary of War, and it became temporarily a part of the First Division.

Prior to our entrance into the war, the regiments of our small army were very much scattered, and we had no organized units, even approximating a division, that could be sent overseas prepared to take the field. To meet the new conditions of warfare an entirely new organization was adopted in which our infantry divisions were to consist of 4 regiments of infantry of about treble their original size, 3 regiments of artillery, 14 machine-gun companies, 1 Engineer regiment, 1 Signal battalion, 1 troop of cavalry, and other auxiliary units, making a total strength of about 28,000 men.

MILITARY SITUATION

3. In order that the reason for many important decisions reached in the early history of the American Expeditionary Forces may be more clearly understood, and the true value of the American effort more fully appreciated, it is desirable to have in mind the main events leading up to the time of our entry into the war.

1914

4. Although the German drive of 1914 had failed in its immediate purpose, yet her armies had made very important gains. German forces were in complete possession of Belgium and occupied rich industrial regions of northern France, embracing one-fourteenth of her population and about three-fourths of her coal and iron. The German armies held a strongly fortified line 468 miles in length, stretching from the Swiss border to Nieuport on the English Channel; her troops were within 48 miles of Paris and the initiative remained in German hands.

In the east the rapidity of the Russian mobilization forced Germany, even before the Battle of the Marne, to send troops to that frontier, but the close of 1914 found the Russian armies ejected from East Prussia and driven back on Warsaw.

* EAST PRUSSIA, POLAND, AND GALICIA

The entry of Turkey into the war, because of the moral effect upon the Moslem world and the immediate constant threat created against Allied communications with the Far East, led to an effort by the Allies in the direction of the Dardanelles.

*NOTE—Maps used are not a part of this report. All are from Progress of Nations (10 Vol. history of the world). Halftones used are not a part of the original report.

1915

5. Italy joined the Allies in May and gave their cause new strength but the effect was more or less offset when Bulgaria entered on the side of the Central Powers.

The threatening situation on the Russian front and in the Balkans was still such that Germany was compelled to exert an immediate offensive effort in those directions and to maintain only a defensive attitude on the western front. German arms achieved a striking series of successes in the vicinity of the Mazurian Lakes and in Galicia, capturing Warsaw, Brest-Litovsk, and Vilna. The Central Powers overran Serbia and Montenegro. Meanwhile, the Italian armies forced Austria to use approximately one-half of her strength against them.

NATIONAL BOUNDARIES AND BATTLE FRONTS, END OF 1915
Occupied territories are shaded

In the west, the French and British launched offensives which cost the German armies considerable loss; but the objectives were limited and the effect was local.

The Dardanelles expedition, having failed in its mission, was withdrawn in January, 1916. In Mesopotamia the Allied operations had not been successful. Although the British fleet had established its superiority on the sea, yet the German submarine blockade had developed into a serious menace to Allied shipping.

1916

6. Germany no doubt believed that her advantage on the eastern

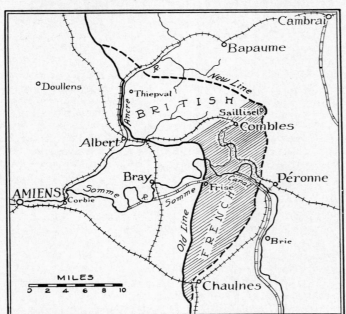

THE BATTLE OF THE SOMME

front at the close of 1915 again warranted an offensive in the west, and her attack against Verdun was accordingly launched in the spring of 1916. But Russia was not yet beaten and early in June, aided at the same time by the threat of an Italian offensive in the west, she began the great drive in Galicia that proved so disastrous to Austria.

Rumania, having entered on the side of the Allies, undertook a promising offensive against Austria. The British and French Armies attacked along the Somme. Germany quickly returned to the defensive in the west, and in September initiated a campaign in the east which, before the close of 1916, proved unfortunate for Russia as well as Rumania.

SPRING OF 1917

7. Retaining on the eastern front the forces considered sufficient for the final conquest of Russia, Germany prepared to aid Austria in an offensive against Italy. Meanwhile, the Russian revolution was well under way and, by the midsummer of 1917, the final collapse of that government was almost certain.

The relatively low strength of the German forces on the western front led the Allies with much confidence to attempt a decision on this front; but the losses were very heavy and the effort signally failed. The failure caused a serious reaction especially on French morale, both in the army and throughout the country, and attempts to carry out extensive or combined operations were indefinitely suspended.

In the five months ending June 30, German submarines had accomplished the destruction of more than three and one-quarter million tons of Allied shipping. During three years Germany had seen practically all her offensives except Verdun crowned with success. Her battle lines were held on foreign soil and she had withstood every Allied attack since the Marne. The German general staff could now foresee the complete elimination of Russia, the possibility of defeating Italy before the end of the year and, finally, the campaign of 1918 against the French and British on the western front which might terminate the war.

NATIONAL BOUNDARIES AND BATTLE FRONTS AT THE END OF 1917
Occupied territories of the combatant Allies are heavily shaded

It can not be said that German hopes of final victory were extravagant, either as viewed at that time or as viewed in the light of history. Financial problems of the Allies were difficult, supplies were becoming exhausted and their armies had suffered tremendous losses. Discouragement existed not only among the civil population but throughout the armies as well. Such was the Allied morale that, although their superiority on the western front during the last half of 1916 and during 1917 amounted to 20 per cent, only local attacks could be undertaken and their effect proved wholly insufficient against the German defense. Allied resources in man power at home were low and there was little prospect of materially increasing their armed strength, even in the face of the probability of having practically the whole military strength of the Central Powers against them in the spring of 1918.

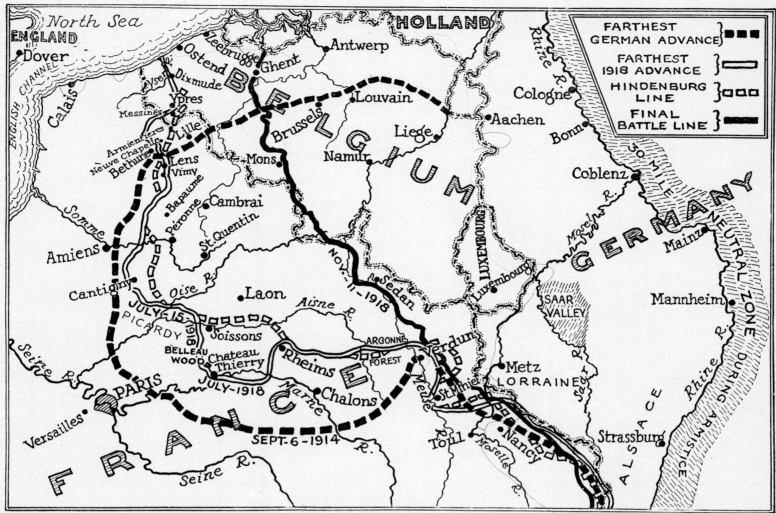

THE WESTERN FRONT

8. This was the state of affairs that existed when we entered the war. While our action gave the Allies much encouragement yet this was temporary, and a review of conditions made it apparent that America must make a supreme material effort as soon as possible. After duly considering the tonnage possibilities I cabled the following to Washington on July 6, 1917:

Plans should contemplate sending over at least 1,000,000 men by next May.

ORGANIZATION PROJECTS

9. A general organization project, covering as far as possible the personnel of all combat, staff, and administrative units, was forwarded to Washington on July 11. This was prepared by the Operations Section of my staff and adopted in joint conference with the War Department Committee then in France. It embodied my conclusions on the military organization and effort required of America after a careful study of French and British experience. In forwarding this project I stated:

It is evident that a force of about 1,000,000 is the smallest unit which in modern war will be a complete, well-balanced, and independent fighting organization. However, it must be equally clear that the adoption of this size force as a basis of study would not be construed as representing the maximum force which should be sent to or which will be needed in France. It is taken as the force which may be expected to reach France in time for an offensive in 1918, and as a unit and basis of organization. Plans

for the future should be based, especially in reference to the manufacture of artillery, aviation, and other material, on three times this force—i. e., at least 3,000,000 men.

The original project for organized combat units and its state of completion on November 11, 1918, are shown in the charts appended to this report. With a few minor changes, this project remained our guide until the end.

10. While this general organization project provided certain Services of Supply troops, which were an integral part of the larger combat units, it did not include the great body of troops and services required to maintain an army overseas. To disembark 2,000,000 men, move them to their training areas, shelter them, handle and store the quantities of supplies and equipment they required called for an extraordinary and immediate effort in construction. To provide the organization for this purpose, a project for engineer services of the rear, including railways, was cabled to Washington August 5, 1917, followed on September 18, 1917, by a complete service of the rear project, which listed item by item the troops considered necessary for the Services of Supply. Particular attention is invited to the charts herewith, which show the extent to which this project had developed by November 11, 1918, and the varied units required, many of which did not exist in our Army prior to this war.

11. In order that the War Department might have a clear-cut program to follow in the shipment of personnel and material to insure the gradual building up of a force at all times balanced and symmetrical, a comprehensive statement was prepared covering the order in which the troops and services enumerated in these two projects should arrive. This schedule of priority of shipments, forwarded to the War Depart-

ment on October 7, divided the initial force called for by the two projects, the service of the rear project, and the schedule of priority of each.

The importance of the three documents, the general organization project, the service of the rear project, and the schedule of priority of shipments should be emphasized, because they formed the basic plan for providing an army in France together with its material for combat, construction, and supply.

AMERICAN FRONT AND LINE OF COMMUNICATIONS

12. Before developing plans for a line of communications it was necessary to decide upon the probable sector of the front for the eventual employment of a distinctive American force. Our mission was offensive and it was essential to make plans for striking the enemy where a definite military decision could be gained. While the Allied Armies had endeavored to maintain the offensive, the British, in order to guard the Channel ports, were committed to operations in Flanders and the French to the portion of the front protecting Paris. Both lacked troops to operate elsewhere on a large scale.

To the east the great fortified district of Verdun and around Metz menaced central France, protected the most exposed portion of the German line of communications, that between Metz and Sedan, and covered the Briey iron region, from which the enemy obtained the greater part of the iron required for munitions and material. The coal fields east of Metz were also covered by these same defenses. A deep advance east of Metz or the capture of the Briey region, by threatening the invasion of rich German territory in the Moselle Valley and the Saar Basin, thus curtailing her supply of coal or iron, would have a decisive effect in forcing a withdrawal of German troops from northern France. The military and economic situation of the enemy, therefore, indicated Lorraine as the field promising the most fruitful results for the employment of our armies.

13. The complexity of trench life had enormously increased the tonnage of supplies required by troops. Not only was it a question of providing food but enormous quantities of munitions and material were needed. Upon the railroads of France fell the burden of meeting the heavy demands of the three and one-half million Allied combatants then engaged.

The British were crowding the Channel ports and the French were exploiting the manufacturing center of Paris, so that the railroads of northern France were already much overtaxed. Even though the Channel ports might be used to a limited extent for shipments through England, the railroads leading eastward would have to cross British and French zones of operations, thus making the introduction of a line of communications based on ports and railways in that region quite impracticable. If the American Army was to have an independent and flexible system it could not use the lines behind the British-Belgian front nor those in rear of the French front covering Paris.

The problem confronting the American Expeditionary Forces was then to superimpose its rail communications on those of France where there would be the least possible disturbance to the arteries of supply of the two great Allied armies already in the field. This would require the utmost use of those lines of the existing French railroad system that could bear an added burden. Double-track railroad lines, from the ports of the Loire and the Gironde Rivers unite at Bourges, running thence via Nevers, Dijon, and Neufchateau, with lines radiating therefrom toward the right wing of the Allied front. It was estimated that these with the collateral lines available, after considerable improvement, could handle an additional 50,000 tons per day, required for an army of 2,000,000 men. The lines selected, therefore, were those leading from the comparatively unused south-Atlantic ports of France to the northeast where it was believed the American Armies could be employed to the best advantage.

14. In the location of our main depots of supply, while it was important that they should be easily accessible, yet they must also be at a safe distance, as we were to meet an aggressive enemy capable of taking the offensive in any one of several directions. The area embracing Tours, Orleans, Montargis, Nevers, and Chateauroux was chosen, as it was centrally located with regard to all points on the arc of the western front.

The ports of St. Nazaire, La Pallice, and Bassens were designated for permanent use, while Nantes, Bordeaux, and Pauillac were for emergency use. Several smaller ports, such as St. Malo, Sables-d'Olonne, and Bayonne, were available chiefly for the importation of coal from England. From time to time, certain trans-Atlantic ships were sent to Le Havre and Cherbourg. In anticipation of a large increase in the amount of tonnage that might be required later, arrangements were made during the German offensive of 1918 to utilize the ports of Marseilles and Toulon as well as other smaller ports on the Mediterranean.

For all practical purposes the American Expeditionary Forces were based on the American Continent. Three thousand miles of ocean to cross with the growing submarine menace confronting us, the quantity of ship tonnage that would be available then unknown and a line of communications by land 400 miles long from French ports to our probable front presented difficulties that seemed almost insurmountable as compared with those of our Allies.

15. For purposes of local administration our line of communications in France was subdivided into districts or sections. The territory corresponding to and immediately surrounding the principal ports were, respectively called base sections, with an intermediate section embracing the region of the great storage depots and an advance section extending to the zone of operations, within which the billeting and training areas for our earlier divisions were located.

16. In providing for the storage and distribution of reserve supplies an allowance of 45 days in the base sections was planned, with 30

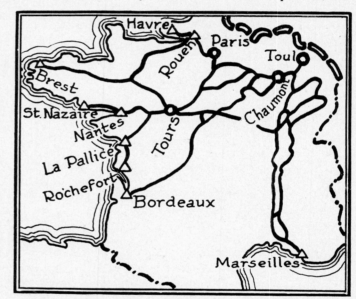

CHIEF SEAPORTS AND LINES OF SUPPLY OF THE A. E. F.

days in the intermediate section and 15 days in the advance section. After the safety of our sea transport was practically assured, this was reduced to a total of 45 days, distributed proportionately. When the Armistice was signed all projects for construction had been completed and supplies were on hand to meet the needs of 2,000,000 men, while further plans for necessary construction and for the supply of an additional 2,000,000 were well under way.

GENERAL STAFF

17. The organization of the General Staff and supply services was one of the first matters to engage my attention. Our situation in this regard was wholly unlike that of our Allies. The French Army was at home and in close touch with its civil government and war department agencies. While the British were organized on an overseas basis, they were within easy reach of their base of supplies in England. Their problems of supply and replacement were simple as compared with ours. Their training could be carried out at home with the experience of the front at hand, while our troops must be sent as ships were provided and their training resumed in France where discontinued

in the States. Our available tonnage was inadequate to meet all the initial demands, so that priority of material for combat and construction, as well as for supplies that could not be purchased in Europe must be established by those whose perspective included all the services and who were familiar with general plans. For the proper direction and coordination of the details of administration, intelligence, operations, supply, and training, a General Staff was an indispensable part of the Army.

The functions of the General Staff at my headquarters were finally allotted to the five sections, each under an Assistant Chief of Staff, as follows: To the First, or Administrative Section—ocean tonnage, priority of overseas shipments, replacement of men and animals, organization and types of equipment for troops, billeting, prisoners of war, military police, leaves and leave areas, welfare work and amusements; to the Second, or Intelligence Section—information regarding the enemy, including espionage and counterespionage, maps, and censorship; to the Third, or Operations Section—strategic studies and plans and employment of combat troops; to the Fourth Section—coordination of supply services, including Construction, Transportation, and Medical Departments, and control of regulating stations for supply; to the Fifth, or Training Section—tactical training, schools, preparation of tactical manuals, and athletics. This same system was applied in the lower echelons of the command down to include divisions, except that in corps and divisions the Fourth Section was merged with the First and the Fifth Section with the Third.

18. As the American Expeditionary Forces grew, it was considered advisable that, in matters of procurement, transportation, and supply, the chiefs of the several supply services, who had hitherto been under the General Staff at my headquarters, should be placed directly under the supervision of the commanding general, Services of Supply. At General Headquarters, a Deputy Chief of Staff to assist the Chief of Staff was provided, and the heads of the five General Staff sections became Assistant Chiefs of Staff.

The General Staff at my headquarters thereafter concerned itself with the broader phase of control. Under my general supervision and pursuant to clearly determined policies, the Assistant Chief of Staff, coordinated by the Chief of Staff, issued instructions and gave general direction to the great combat units and to the Services of Supply, keeping always in close touch with the manner and promptness of their fulfillment. Thus a system of direct responsibility was put into operation which contemplated secrecy in preparation, prompt decision in emergency, and coordinate action in execution.

19. With the growth of our forces the demand for staff officers rapidly increased, but the available number of officers trained for staff duty was very limited. To meet this deficiency, a General Staff college was organized at Langres on November 28, 1917, for the instruction of such officers as could be spared. An intensive course of study of three months was prescribed embracing the details of our staff organization, and administration, and our system of supply, and teaching the combined employment of all arms and services in combat. Officers were carefully chosen for their suitability and, considering the short time available graduates from this school returned well equipped for staff duties and with a loyal spirit of common service much accentuated. The Staff College carried to completion four courses of three months each, graduating 537 staff officers.

TRAINING FOR WAR

20. Soon after our arrival in Europe careful study was made of the methods followed by our Allies in training combat troops. Both the French and British maintained continuously a great system of schools and training centers, which provided for both theoretical and practical instruction of inexperienced officers and noncomissioned officers. These centers were required not only to train new troops, but to prepare officers and soldiers for advancement by giving them a short course in the duties of their new grades. These schools systems made it possible to spread rapidly a knowledge of the latest methods developed by experience and at the same time counteract false notions.

21. A similar scheme was adopted in August, 1917, for our Armies in which the importance of teaching throughout our forces a sound fighting doctrine of our own was emphasized. It provided for troop training in all units up to include divisions. Corps centers of instruction for noncommissioned officers and unit commanders of all arms were established. These centers also provided special training for the instructors needed at corps schools. Base training centers for replacement troops and special classes of soldiers, such as cooks and mechanics, were designated. The army and corps schools were retained under the direct supervision of the Training Section, General Staff. The schools mentioned graduated 21,330 noncommissioned officers and 13,916 officers.

Particular care was taken to search the ranks for the most promising soldiers, in order to develop leaders for the command of platoons and companies. There were graduated from these candidate schools in France 10,976 soldiers. It was planned to have 22,000 infantrymen under instruction by January 1, 1919, graduating 5,000 to 6,000 each month. In addition, there were to be graduated monthly 800 artillery men, 400 engineers, and 200 signalmen, making a total of about 7,000 soldiers each month. Prior to November 14, 1918, 12,732 soldiers were commissioned as officers.

It must not be thought that such a system is ideal, but it represents a compromise between the demand for efficiency and the imperative and immediate necessity for trained replacement officers.

22. Every advantage was taken of the experience of our Allies in training officers. It was early recommended to the War Department that French and British officers be asked for to assist in the instruction of troops in the United States. Pending the organization and development of our own schools, a large number of our officers were sent to centers of instruction of the Allied armies. The training of our earlier divisions was begun in close association with the French divisions, under conditions set forth in the following paragraph on divisional training:

Trench warfare naturally gives prominence to the defensive as opposed to the offensive. To guard against this, the basis of instruction should be essentially the offensive both in spirit and in practice. The defensive is accepted only to prepare for future offensive.

For training our Artillery units, special localities such as Valdahon, Coetquidan, Meucon, and Souge, had to be sought, and the instruction was usually carried on in conjunction with French artillery followed up later, as far as possible, with field practice in cooperation with our own infantry.

23. The long period of trench warfare had so impressed itself upon the French and British that they had almost entirely dispensed with training for open warfare. It was to avoid this result in our Army and to encourage the offensive spirit that the following was published in October, 1917:

1 * * * (a) The above methods to be employed must remain or become distinctly our own.

(b) All instruction must contemplate the assumption of a vigorous offensive. This purpose will be emphasized in every phase of training until it becomes a settled habit of thought.

(c) The general principles governing combat remain unchanged in their essence. This war has developed special features which involve special phases of training, but the fundamental ideas enunciated in our Drill Regulations, Small Arms Firing Manual, Field Service Regulations, and other service manuals remain the guide for both officers and soldiers and constitute the standard by which their efficiency is to be measured, except as modified in detail by instruction from these headquarters.

(d) The rifle and the bayonet are the principal weapons of the infantry soldier. He will be trained to a high degree of skill as a marksman, both on the target range and in the field firing. An aggressive spirit must be developed until the soldier feels himself, as a bayonet fighter, invincible in battle.

(e) All officers and soldiers should realize that at no time in our history has discipline been so important; therefore, discipline of the highest order must be exacted at all times. The standards for the American Army will be those of West Point. The rigid attention, upright bearing, attention to detail, uncomplaining obedience to instructions required of the cadet will be required of every officer and soldier of our armies in France. * * *

Recommendations were cabled to Washington emphasizing the importance of target practice and musketry training, and recommending that instruction in open warfare be made the mission of troops in the United States, while the training in trench warfare so far as necessary be conducted in France. Succeeding divisions, whether serving temporarily with the British or French, were trained as thus indicated. The assistance of the French units was limited to demonstrations, and, in the beginning French instructors taught the use of French arms and assisted in the preparation of elementary trench warfare problems.

Assuming that divisions would arrive with their basic training completed in the United States, one month was allotted for the instruction of small units from battalions down, a second month of experience in quiet sectors by battalions, and a third month for field practice in open warfare tactics by division, including artillery. Unfortunately many divisions did not receive the requisite amount of systematic training before leaving the States and complete preparation of such units for battle was thus often seriously delayed.

24. The system of training profoundly influenced the combat efficiency of our troops by its determined insistence upon an offensive doctrine and upon training in warfare movement. Instruction which had hitherto been haphazard, varying with the ideas and conceptions of inexperienced commanding officers and indifferent instructors, was brought under a system based on correct principles. Approved and systematic methods were maintained and enforced largely by the continual presence of members of the Training Section with the troops both during the training period and in campaign.

ESPIONAGE SYSTEMS

25. Before our entry into the war, European experience had shown that military operations can be carried out successfully and without unnecessary loss only in the light of complete and reliable information of the enemy. Warfare with battle lines separated by short distances only, made possible the early acquirement of information, such as that obtained through airplane photography, observation from balloons and planes, sensitive instruments for detecting gun positions and raids to secure prisoners and documents. All such information, together with that from Allied sources, including military, political, and economical, was collected, classified, and rapidly distributed where needed.

---

26. From careful studies of the systems and actual participation by our officers in methods in use at various Allied headquarters, an Intelligence Service was evolved in our forces which operated successfully from its first organization in August, 1917.

With us the simpler methods, such as observation from the air and ground and the exploitation of prisoners and documents, have proved more effective than the less direct means. Every unit from the battalion up had an intelligence department, but only in divisions and larger organizations did the intelligence agencies embrace all available means and sources, including radio interception stations and sound and flash-ranging detachments.

27. The subjects studied by the Intelligence Section embraced the location of the enemy's front line, his order of battle, the history and fighting value of his divisions, his manpower, his combat activities, circulation and movement, his defensive organizations, supply, construction and material, air service, radio service, strategy and tactics, and what he probably knew of our intentions. The political and economic conditions within the enemy's countries were also of extreme importance.

28. To disseminate conclusions, daily publications were necessary, such as a Secret Summary of Intelligence containing information of the broadest scope, which concerned only General Headquarters; and a Summary of Information, distributed down to include the divisions, giving information affecting the western front. A Press Review and a Summary of Air Intelligence were also published.

Maps showing graphically the disposition and movement of enemy troops in our front were the best means for distributing information to our troops. At the base printing plant and at General Headquarters base maps were prepared while mobile printing plants, mounted on trucks, accompanied corps and army headquarters. Combat troops were thus supplied with excellent maps distributed, just before and during an attack, down to include company and platoon commanders. Between July 1 and November 11, 1918, over 5,000,000 maps were used.

29. The secret service, espionage and counterespionage, was organized in close cooperation with the French and British. To prevent indiscretions in the letters of officers and soldiers, as well as in articles written for the press, the Censorship Division was created. The Base Censor examined individual letters when the writer so desired, censored all mail written in foreign languages, of which there were over 50 used, and frequently checked up letters of entire organizations.

30. The policy of press censorship adopted aimed to accomplish three broad results:

To prevent the enemy from obtaining important information of our forces.

To give to the people of the United States the maximum information consistent with the limitations imposed by the first object.

To cause to be presented to the American people the facts as they were known at the time.

There were with our forces 36 regularly accredited correspondents, while visiting correspondents reached a total of 411.

SUMMER OF 1917 TO SPRING OF 1918

31. In order to hinder the enemy's conquest of Russia and, if possible, prevent a German attack on Italy, or in the near east, the Allies sought to maintain the offensive on the western front as far as their diminished strength and morale would permit. On June 7, 1917, the British took Messines, while a succession of operations known as the Third Battle of Ypres began on July 31 and terminated with the capture of the Passchendaele Ridge November 6-10. The British attack at Cambrai is of special interest, since it was here that American troops (Eleventh Engineers) first participated in active fighting.

The French successfully attacked on a limited front near Verdun, capturing Mort Homme on August 20 and advancing their lines to La Forge Brook. In another offensive, begun on October 23, they gained considerable ground on Chemin des Dames Ridge. These French attacks were characterized by most careful preparation to insure success in order to improve the morale of their troops.

32. Notwithstanding these Allied attacks on the western front, the immense gains by the German armies in the east, culminating at Riga on September 3, precipitated the collapse of Russia. The following month, the Austrians with German assistance surprised the Italians and broke through the lines at Caporetto, driving the Italian armies back to the Piave River, inflicting a loss of 300,000 men, 600,000 rifles, 3,000 guns, and enormous stores. This serious crisis compelled the withdrawal of 10 French and British divisions from the western front to Italy. The German situation on all other theaters was so favorable that as early as November they began the movement of divisions toward the western front. If needed, her divisions could be withdrawn from the Italian front before the French and British dared recall their divisions.

33. At first the Allies could hardly hope for a large American Army. Marshall Joffre during his visit to America had made special request that a combat division be sent at once to Europe as visual evidence of our purpose to participate actively in the war, and also asked for Engineer regiments and other special service units.

The arrival of the First Division and the parade of certain of its elements in Paris on July 4 caused great enthusiasm and for the time being French morale was stimulated. Still Allied apprehension was deep-seated and material assistance was imperative. The following extract is quoted from the cabled summary of an Allied conference held on July 26 with the French and Italian Commanders-in-Chief and the British and French Chiefs of Staff:

General conclusions reached were necessity for adoption of purely defensive attitude on all secondary fronts and withdrawing surplus troops for duty on western front. By thus strengthening western front believed Allies could hold until American forces arrive in numbers sufficient to gain ascendency.

The conference urged the immediate study of the tonnage situation with a view to accelerating the arrival of American troops. With the approach of winter, depression among the Allies over the Russian collapse and the Italian crisis was intensified by the conviction that the Germans would undertake a decisive offensive in the spring.

A review of the situation showed that with Russia out of the war the Central Powers would be able to release a large number of divisions for service elsewhere, and that during the spring and summer of 1918, without interfering with the status quo at Salonika, they could concentrate on the western front a force much stronger than that of the Allies. In view of this, it was represented to the War Department in December as of the utmost importance that the Allied preparations be expedited.

34. On December 31, 1917, there were 176,665 American troops in France and but one division had appeared on the front. Disappointment at the delay of the American effort soon began to develop. French and British authorities suggested the more rapid entry of our troops into the line and urged the amalgamation of our troops with their own, even insisting upon the curtailment of training to conform to the strict minimum of trench requirements they considered necessary.

My conclusion was that, although the morale of the German people and of the armies was better than it had been for two years, only an untoward combination of circumstances could give the enemy a decisive victory before American support as recommended could be made effective, provided the Allies secured unity of action. However, a situation might arise which would necessitate the temporary use of all American troops in the units of our Allies for the defensive, but nothing in the situation justified the relinquishment of our firm purpose to form our own Army under our own flag.

While the Germans were practicing for open warfare and concentrating their most aggressive personnel in shock divisions, the training of the Allies was still limited to trench warfare. As our troops were being trained for open warfare, there was every reason why we could not allow them to be scattered among our Allies, even by divisions, much less as replacements, except by pressure of sheer necessity. Any sort of permanent amalgamation would irrevocably commit America's fortunes to the hands of the Allies. Moreover it was obvious that the lack of homogeneity would render these mixed divisions difficult to maneuver and almost certain to break up under stress of defeat, with the consequent mutual recrimination. Again there was no doubt that the realization by the German people that independent American divisions, corps, or armies were in the field with determined purpose would be a severe blow to German morale and prestige.

It was also certain that an early appearance of the larger American units on the front would be most beneficial to the morale of the Allies themselves. Accordingly, the First Division, on January 19, 1918, took over a sector north of Toul; the Twenty-sixth Division went to the Soissons front early in February; the Forty-second Division entered the line near Luneville, February 21, and the Second Division near Verdun, March 18. Meanwhile, the First Army Corps Headquarters, Maj. Gen. Hunter Liggett, commanding, was organized at Neufchateau on January 20, and the plan to create an independent American sector on the Lorraine front was taking shape.

This was the situation when the great German offensive was launched on March 21, 1918.

Part II.

Operations

Expediting Shipment of Troops

1. The War Department planned as early as July, 1917, to send to France by June 15, 1918, 21 divisions of the then strength of 20,000 men each, together with auxiliary and replacement troops, and those needed for the line of communications, amounting to over 200,000, making a total of some 650,000 men. Beginning with October 6, divisions were to be sent during that quarter, 7 during the first quarter of 1918, and 8 the second quarter. While these numbers fell short of my recommendation of July 6, 1917, which contemplated at least 1,000,000 men by May, 1918, it should be borne in mind that the main factor in the problem was the amount of shipping to become available for military purposes, in which must be included tonnage required to supply the Allies with steel, coal, and food.

2. On December 2, 1917, an estimate of the situation was cabled to the War Department with the following recommendation:

Paragraph 3. In view of these conditions, it is of the utmost importance to the Allied cause that we move swiftly The minimum number of troops we should plan to have in France by the end of June is 4 Army corps of 24 divisions in addition to troops for service of the rear. Have impressed the present urgency upon Gen. Bliss and other American members of the conference. Gens. Robertson, Foch, and Bliss agree with me that this is the minimum that should be aimed at. This figure is given as the lowest we should think of and is placed no higher because the limit of available transportation would not seem to warrant it.

Paragraph 4. A study of transportation facilities shows sufficient American tonnage to bring over this number of troops, but to do so there must be a reduction in the tonnage allotted to other than Army needs. It is estimated that the shipping needed will have to be rapidly increased up to 2,000,000 tons by May, in addition to the amount already allotted. The use of shipping for commercial purposes must be curtailed as much as possible. The Allies are very weak and we must come to their relief this

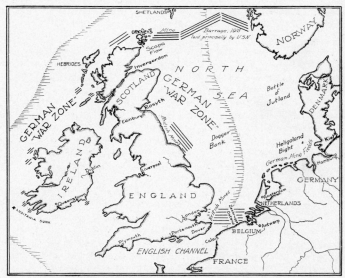

NAVAL OPERATIONS IN THE NORTH SEA

year, 1918. The year after may be too late. It is very doubtful if they can hold on until 1919 unless we give them a lot of support this year. It is therefore strongly recommended that a complete readjustment of transportation be made and that the needs of the War Department as set forth above be regarded as immediate. Further details of these requirements will be sent later.

and again on December 20, 1917:

Understood here that a shipping program based on tonnage in sight prepared in War College Division in September contem-

THE ZERO HOUR IN THE TRENCHES

plated that entire First Corps with its corps troops and some 32,000 auxiliaries were to have been shipped by end of November, and that an additional program for December, January, and February contemplates that the shipment of the Second Corps with its corps troops and other auxiliaries should be practically completed by the end of February. Should such a program be carried out as per schedule and should shipments continue at corresponding rate, it would not succeed in placing even three complete corps, with proper proportion of Army troops and auxiliaries, in France by the end of May. The actual facts are that shipments are not even keeping up to that schedule. It is now the middle of December and the First Corps is still incomplete by over two entire divisions * and many corps troops. It can not be too emphatically declared that we should be prepared to take the field with at least four corps by June 30. In view of past performances with tonnage heretofore available such a project is impossible of fulfillment, but only by most strenuous attempts to attain such a result will we be in a position to take a proper part in operations in 1918. In view of fact that as the number of our troops here increases a correspondingly greater amount of tonnage must be provided for their supply, and also in view of the slow rate of shipment with tonnage now available, it is of the most urgent importance that more tonnage should be obtained at once as already recommended in my cables and by Gen. Bliss.

3. During January, 1918, discussions were held with the British authorities that resulted in an agreement, which became known as the six-division plan and which provided for the transportation of six entire divisions in British tonnage, without interference with our own shipping program. High commanders, staff, infantry, and auxiliary troops were to be given experience with British divisions, beginning with battalions, the artillery to be trained under American direction, using French matériel. It was agreed that when sufficiently trained these battalions were to be re-formed into regiments and that when the artillery was fully trained all of the units comprising each division were to be united for service under their own officers. It was planned that the period of training with the British should cover about 10 weeks. To supervise the administration and training of these divisions the Second Corps staff was organized February 20, 1918.

In the latter part of January joint note No. 12, presented by the Military Representatives with the Supreme War Council was approved by the Council. This note concluded that France would be safe during 1918 only under certain conditions, namely:

(a) That the strength of the British and French troops in France is continuously kept up to their present total strength and that they receive the expected reinforcements of not less than two American divisions per month.

THE GERMAN OFFENSIVES OF 1918 AND RELATED ALLIED AGREEMENTS

4. The first German offensive of 1918, beginning March 21, overran all resistance during the initial period of the attack. Within eight days the enemy had completely crossed the old Somme battlefield and had swept everything before him to a depth of some 56 kilometers. For a few days the loss of the railroad center of Amiens appeared imminent. The offensive made such inroads upon French and British reserves that defeat stared them in the face unless the new American troops should prove more immediately available than even the most optimistic had dared to hope. On March 27 the Military Representatives with the Supreme War Council prepared their joint note No. 18. This note repeated the previously quoted statement from joint note No. 12, and continued:

The battle which is developing at the present moment in France and which can extend to the other theaters of operations, may very quickly place the Allied Armies in a serious situation from the point of view of effectives, and the Military Representatives are from this moment of opinion that the above-detailed condition (see (a) par. 3) can no longer be maintained, and they

*The First, Forty-second, Second, and Twenty-sixth Division had arrived; but not the Replacement and the Depot Division.

THE 28TH INF. JUMP-OFF AT CANTIGNY. THE RESULT OF AMERICA'S FIRST TASTE OF FIRE WAS ANXIOUSLY AWAITED BY THE ALLIES WHOSE EBBING MORALE WAS GREATLY STRENGTHENED BY THE VICTORY.

consider as a general proposition that the new situation requires new decisions.

The Military Representatives are of opinion that it is highly desirable that the American Government should assist the Allied Armies as soon as possible by permitting in principle the temporary service of American units in Allied Army corps and divisions. Such reinforcements must, however, be obtained from other units than those American divisions which are now operating with the French, and the units so temporarily employed must eventually be returned to the American Army.

The Military Representatives are of the opinion that from the present time, in execution of the foregoing, and until otherwise directed by the Supreme War Council, only American infantry and machine-gun units, organized as that Government may decide, be brought to France, and that all agreements or conventions hitherto made in conflict with this decision be modified accordingly.

The Secretary of War, who was in France at this time, Gen. Bliss, the American Military Representative with the Supreme War Council, and I at once conferred on the terms of this note, with the result that the Secretary recommended to the President that joint note No. 18 be approved in the following sense:

The purpose of the American Government is to render the fullest cooperation and aid, and therefore the recommendation of the Military Representatives with regard to the preferential transportation of American infantry and machine-gun units in the present emergency is approved. Such units, when transported, will be under the direction of the Commander-in-Chief of the American Expeditionary Forces, and will be assigned for training and use by him in his discretion. He will use these and all other military forces of the United States under his command in such manner as to render the greatest military assistance, keeping in mind always the determination of this Government to have its various military forces collected, as speedily as their training and the military situation permits, into an independent American Army, acting in concert with the armies of Great Britain and France, and all arrangements made by him for their temporary training and service will be made with that end in view.

While note No. 18 was general in its terms, the priority of shipments of infantry more especially pertained to those divisions that were to be trained in the British area, as that Government was to provide the additional shipping according to the six-division plan agreed upon even before the beginning of the March 21 offensive.

On April 2 the War Department cabled that preferential transportation would be given to American infantry and machine-gun units during the existing emergency. Preliminary arrangements were made for training and early employment with the French of such infantry units as might be sent over by our own transportation. As for the British agreement, the six-division plan was to be modified to give priority to the infantry of those divisions. However, all the Allies were now urging the indefinite continuation of priority for the shipment of infantry and its complete incorporation in their units, which fact was cabled to the War Department on April 3, with the specific recommendation that the total immediate priority of infantry be limited to four divisions, plus 45,500 replacements, and that the necessity for future priority be determined later.

5. The Secretary of War and I held a conference with British authorities on April 7, during which it developed that the British had erroneously assumed that the preferential shipment of infantry was to be continuous. It was agreed at this meeting that 60,000 infantry and machine-gun troops, with certain auxiliary units to be brought over by British tonnage during April, should go to the British area as part of the six-division plan, but that there should be a further agreement as to subsequent troops to be brought over by the British. Consequently, a readjustment of the priority schedule was undertaken on the basis of postponing "shipment of all noncombatant troops to the utmost possible to meet present situation, and at the same time not make it impossible to build up our own Army."

6. The battle line in the vicinity of Amiens had hardly stabilized when, on April 9, the Germans made another successful attack against the British lines on a front of some 40 kilometers in the vicinity of

Armentieres and along the Lys River. As a result of its being included in a salient formed by the German advance, Passchendaele Ridge, the capture of which had cost so dearly in 1917, was evacuated by the British on April 17.

The losses had been heavy and the British were unable to replace them entirely. They were, therefore, making extraordinary efforts to increase the shipping available for our troops. On April 21, I went to London to clear up certain questions concerning the rate of shipment and to reach the further agreement provided for in the April 7 conference. The result of this London agreement was cabled to Washington April 24, as follows:

(a) That only the infantry, machine guns, engineers and signal troops of American divisions and the headquarters of divisions and brigades be sent over in British and American shipping during May for training and service with the British army in France up to six divisions and that any shipping in excess of that required for these troops be utilized to transport troops necessary to make these divisions complete. The training and service of these troops will be carried out in accordance with plans already agreed upon between Sir Douglas Haig and Gen. Pershing, with a view at an early date of building up American divisions.

(b) That the American personnel of the artillery of these divisions and such corps troops as may be required to build up American corps organizations follow immediately thereafter, and that American artillery personnel be trained with French matériel and join its proper divisions as soon as thoroughly trained.

(c) If, when the program outlined in paragraphs (a) and (b) is completed, the military situation makes advisable the further shipment of infantry, etc., of American divisions, then all the British and American shipping available for transport of troops shall be used for that purpose under such arrangement as will insure immediate aid to the Allies, and at the same time provide at the earliest moment for bringing over American artillery and other necessary units to complete the organization of American divisions and corps. Provided that the combatant troops mentioned in (a) and (b) be followed by such Service of the Rear and other troops as may be considered necessary by the American Commander-in-Chief.

(d) That it is contemplated American divisions and corps when trained and organized shall be utilized under the American Commander-in-Chief in an American group.

(e) That the American Commander-in-Chief shall allot American troops to the French or British for training or train them with American units at his discretion, with the understanding that troops already transported by British shipping or included in the six divisions mentioned in paragraph (a) are to be trained with the British Army, details as to rations, equipment, and transport to be determined by special agreement.

7. At a meeting of the Supreme War Council held at Abbeville May 1 and 2, the entire question of the amalgamation of Americans with the French and British was reopened. An urgent appeal came from both French and Italian representatives for American replacements or units to serve with their armies. After prolonged discussion regarding this question and that of priority generally the following agreement was reached, committing the Council to an independent American Army and providing for the immediate shipment of certain troops:

It is the opinion of the Supreme War Council that, in order to carry the war to a successful conclusion, an American Army should be formed as early as possible under its own commander and under its own flag. In order to meet the present emergency it is agreed that American troops should be brought to France as rapidly as Allied transportation facilities will permit, and that, as far as consistent with the necessity of building up an American Army, preference will be given to infantry and machine-gun units for training and service with the French and British Armies; with the understanding that such infantry and machine-gun units are to be withdrawn and united with its own artillery and auxiliary troops into divisions and corps at the direction of the American Commander-in-Chief after consultation with the Commander-in-Chief of the Allied Armies in France.

Subparagraph A. It is also agreed that during the month of May preferences should be given to the transportation of infantry and machine-gun units of six divisions, and that any excess tonnage shall be devoted to bringing over such other troops as may be determined by the American Commander-in-Chief.

Subparagraph B. It is further agreed that this program shall be continued during the month of June upon condition that the British Government shall furnish transportation for a minimum of 130,000 men in May and 150,000 men in June, with the understanding that the first six divisions of infantry shall go to the British for training and service, and that troops sent over in June shall be allocated for training and service as the American Commander-in-Chief may determine.

Subparagraph C. It is also further agreed that if the British Government shall transport an excess of 150,000 men in June that such excess shall be infantry and machine-gun units, and that early in June there shall be a new review of the situation to determine further action.

GERMAN OFFENSIVE DRIVES OF 1918

The gravity of the situation had brought the Allies to a full realization of the necessity of providing all possible tonnage for the transportation of American troops. Although their views were accepted to the extent of giving a considerable priority to infantry and machine gunners, the priority agreed upon as to this class of troops was not as extensive as some of them deemed necessary, and the Abbeville conference was adjourned with the understanding that the question of further priority would be discussed at a conference to be held about the end of May.

8. The next offensive of the enemy was made between the Oise and Berry-au-Bac against the French instead of against the British, as was generally expected, and it came as a complete surprise. The initial Aisne attack, covering a front of 35 kilometers, met with remarkable success, as the German armies advanced no less than 50 kilometers in four days. On reaching the Marne that river was used as a defensive flank and the German advance was directed toward Paris. During the

A 42ND DIVISION (SERVING WITH FR.) OUTPOST IN THE WOODS OF PARRON EAST OF LUNEVILLE MARCH 5, 1918.
A FEW MINUTES AFTER THE PICTURE WAS TAKEN THE POSITION WAS BLOWN UP BY ENEMY SHELL FIRE.

first days of June something akin to a panic seized the city and it was estimated that 1,000,000 people left during the spring of 1918.

The further conference which had been agreed upon at Abbeville was held at Versailles on June 1 and 2. The opinion of our Allies as to the existing situation and the urgency of their insistence upon further priority for infantry and machine gunners are shown by the following message prepared by the Prime Ministers of Great Britain, France, and Italy, and agreed to by Gen. Foch:

The Prime Ministers of France, Italy, and Great Britain, now meeting at Versailles, desire to send the following message to the President of the United States:

"We desire to express our warmest thanks to President Wilson for the remarkable promptness with which American aid, in excess of what at one time seemed practicable, has been rendered to the Allies during the past month to meet a great emergency. The crisis, however, still continues. Gen. Foch has presented to us a statement of the utmost gravity, which points out that the numerical superiority of the enemy in France, where 162 Allied divisions now oppose 200 German divisions, is very heavy, and that, as there is no possibility of the British and French increasing the number of their divisions (on the contrary, they are put to extreme straits to keep them up) there is a great danger of the war being lost unless the numerical inferiority of the Allies can be remedied as rapidly as possible by the advent of American troops. He, therefore, urges with the utmost insistence that the maximum possible number of infantry and machine gunners, in which respect the shortage of men on the side of the Allies is most marked, should continue to be shipped from America in the months of June and July to avert the immediate danger from an Allied defeat in the present campaign owing to the Allied reserves being exhausted before those of the enemy. In addition to this, and looking to the future, he represents that it is impossible to foresee ultimate victory in the war unless America is able to provide such an Army as will enable the Allies ultimately to establish numerical superiority. He places the total American force required for this at no less than 100 divisions, and urges the continuous raising of fresh American levies, which, in his opinion, should not be less than 300,000 a month, with a view to establishing a total American force of 100 divisions at as early a date as this can possibly be done.

"We are satisfied that Gen. Foch, who is conducting the present campaign with consummate ability, and on whose military judgment we continue to place the most absolute reliance, is not over-estimating the needs of the case, and we feel confident that the Government of the United States will do everything that can be done, both to meet the needs of the immediate situation and to proceed with the continuous raising of fresh levies, calculated to provide, as soon as possible, the numerical superiority which the Commander-in-Chief of the Allied Armies regards as essential to ultimate victory.

"A separate telegram contains the arrangements which Gen. Foch, Gen. Pershing, and Lord Milner have agreed to recommend to the United States Government with regard to the dispatch of American troops for the months of June and July.

(Signed) "CLEMENCEAU, "D. LLOYD GEORGE, "ORLANDO."

Such extensive priority had already been given to the transport of American infantry and machine gunners that the troops of those categories which had received even partial training in the United States were practically exhausted. Moreover, the strain on our Services of Supply made it essential that early relief be afforded by increasing its personnel. At the same time, the corresponding services of our Allies had in certain departments been equally overtaxed and their responsible heads were urgent in their representations that their needs must be relieved by bringing over American specialists. The final agreement was cabled to the War Department on June 5, as follows:

The following agreement has been concluded between Gen. Foch, Lord Milner, and myself with reference to the transportation of American troops in the months of June and July:

"The following recommendations are made on the assumption that at least 250,000 men can be transported in each of the months of June and July by the employment of combined British and American tonnage. We recommend:

"(a) For the month of June: (1) Absolute priority shall be given to the transportation of 170,000 combatant troops (viz, six divisions without artillery, ammunition trains, or supply trains, amounting to 126,000 men and 44,000 replacements for combat troops); (2) 25,400 men for the service of the railways, of which 13,400 have been asked for by the French Minister of Transportation; (3) the balance to be troops of categories to be determined by the Commander-in-Chief, American Expeditionary Forces.

"(b) For the month of July: (1) Absolute priority for the shipment of 140,000 combatant troops of the nature defined above (four divisions minus artillery 'et cetera' amounting to 84,000 men, plus 56,000 replacement); (2) the balance of the 250,000 to consist of troops to be designated by the Commander-in-Chief, American Expeditionary Forces.

"(c) It is agreed that if the available tonnage in either month allows of the transportation of a larger number of men than 250,-000, the excess tonnage will be employed in the transportation of combat troops as defined above.

"(d) We recognize that the combatant troops to be dispatched in July may have to include troops which have had insufficient training, but we consider the present emergency is such as to justify a temporary and exceptional departure by the United States from sound principles of training, especially as a similar course is being followed by France and Great Britain.

(Signed) "Foch,
"Milner,
"Pershing."

9. The various proposals during these conferences regarding priority of shipment, often very insistent, raised questions that were not only most difficult but most delicate. On the one hand, there was a critical situation which must be met by immediate action, while, on the other hand, any priority accorded a particular arm necessarily postponed the formation of a distinctive American fighting force and the means to supply it. Such a force was, in my opinion, absolutely necessary to win the war. A few of the Allied representatives became convinced that the American Services of Supply should not be neglected but should be developed in the common interest. The success of our divisions during May and June demonstrated fully that it was not necessary to draft Americans under foreign flags in order to utilize American manhood most effectively.

ALLIED COMMANDER-IN-CHIEF

10. When, on March 21, 1918, the German Army on the western front began its series of offensives, it was by far the most formidable force the world had ever seen. In fighting men and guns it had a great superiority, but this was of less importance than the advantage in

FIRING A STOKES MORTAR: CHEMICAL WARFARE SERVICE, CHAUMONT, HTE. MARNE, FRANCE, OCT. 16, 1918.

morale, in experience, in training for mobile warfare, and in unity of command. Ever since the collapse of the Russian armies and the crisis on the Italian front in the fall of 1917, German armies were being assembled and trained for the great campaign which was to end the war before America's effort could be brought to bear. Germany's best troops, her most successful generals, and all the experience gained in three years of war were mobilized for the supreme effort.

The first blow fell on the right of the British Armies, including the junction of the British and French forces. Only the prompt cooperation of the French and British general headquarters stemmed the tide. The reason for this objective was obvious and strikingly illustrated the necessity for having someone with sufficient authority over all the Allied Armies to meet such an emergency. The lack of complete cooperation among the Allies on the western front had been appreciated and the question of preparation to meet a crisis had already received attention by the Supreme War Council. A plan had been adopted by which each of the Allies would furnish a certain number of divisions for a general reserve to be under the direction of the military representatives of the Supreme War Council of which Gen. Foch was then the senior member. But when the time came to meet the German offensive in March these reserves were not found available and the plan failed.

This situation resulted in a conference for the immediate consideration of the question of having an Allied Commander-in-Chief. After much discussion during which my view favoring such action was clearly stated, an agreement was reached and Gen. Foch was selected. His appointment as such was made April 3 and was approved for the United States by the President on April 16. The terms of the agreement under which Gen. Foch exercised his authority were as follows:

BEAUVAIS, *April 3, 1918.*

Gen. Foch is charged by the British, French, and American Governments with the coordination of the action of the Allied Armies on the western front; to this end there is conferred on him all the powers necessary for its effective realization. To the same end, the British, French, and American Governments confide in Gen. Foch the strategic direction of military operations.

The Commander-in-Chief of the British, French, and American Armies will exercise to the fullest extent the tactical direction of their armies. Each Commander-in-Chief will have the right to appeal to his Government, if in his opinion his Army is placed in danger by the instructions received from Gen. Foch.

(Signed) G. CLEMENCEAU.
PETAIN.
F. FOCH.
LLOYD GEORGE.
D. HAIG, *F. M.*
HENRY WILSON, *General, 3.4.18.*
TASKER H. BLISS, *General and Chief of Staff.*
JOHN J. PERSHING, *General, U. S. A.*

The American Divisions In Action

11. The grave crisis precipitated by the first German offensive caused me to make a hurried visit to Gen. Foch's headquarters, at Bombon, during which all our combatant forces were placed at his disposal. The acceptance of this offer meant the dispersion of our troops along the Allied front and a consequent delay in building up a distinctive American force in Lorraine, but the serious situation of the Allies demanded this divergence from our plans.

On March 21, approximately 300,000 American troops had reached France. Four combat divisions, equivalent in strength to eight French or British divisions, were available—the First and Second then in line, and the Twenty-sixth and Forty-second just withdrawn from line after one month's trench warfare training. The last two divisions at once began taking over quiet sectors to release divisions for the battle; the Twenty-sixth relieved the First Division, which was sent to northwest of Paris in reserve; the Forty-second relieved two French divisions from quiet sectors. In addition to these troops, one regiment of the Ninety-third Division was with the French in the Argonne, the Forty-first Depot Division was in the Services of Supply, and three divisions (Third, Thirty-second, and Fifth) were arriving.

12. On April 25 the First Division relieved two French divisions on the front near Montdidier and on May 28 captured the important observation stations on the heights of Cantigny with splendid dash. French artillery, aviation, tanks, and flame throwers aided in the attack, but most of this French assistance was withdrawn before the completion of the operation in order to meet the enemy's new offensive launched May 27 toward Chateau-Thierry. The enemy's reaction against our troops at Cantigny was extremely violent, and apparently he was determined at all costs to counteract the most excellent effect the American success had produced. For three days his guns of all calibers were concentrated on our new position and counterattack succeeded counterattack. The desperate efforts of the Germans gave the fighting at Cantigny a seeming tactical importance entirely out of proportion to the numbers involved.

13. Of the three divisions arriving in France when the first German offensive began, the Thirty-second, intended for replacements, had been temporarily employed in the Services of Supply to meet a shortage of personnel, but the critical situation caused it to be reassembled and by May 21 it was entering the line in the Vosges. At this time the Fifth Division, though still incomplete, was also ordered into the line in the same region. The Third Division was assembling in its training area and the Third Corps staff had just been organized to administer these three divisions. In addition to the eight divisions already mentioned, the Twenty-eighth and Seventy-seventh had arrived in the British area, and the Fourth, Twenty-seventh, Thirtieth, Thirty-third, Thirty-fifth, and Eighty-second were arriving there. Following the agreements as to British shipping, our troops came so rapidly that by the end of May we had a force of 600,000 in France.

The Third German offensive on May 27, against the French on the Aisne, soon developed a desperate situation for the Allies. The Second Division, then in reserve northwest of Paris and preparing to relieve the First Division, was hastily diverted to the vicinity of Meaux on May 31, and, early on the morning of June 1, was deployed across the Chateau-Thierry-Paris road near Montreuil-aux-Lions in a gap in the French line, where it stopped the German advance on Paris. At the same time the partially trained Third Division was placed at French disposal to hold the crossings of the Marne, and its motorized machine-gun battalion succeeded in reaching Chateau-Thierry in time to assist in successfully defending that river crossing.

The enemy having been halted, the Second Division commenced a series of vigorous attacks on June 4, which resulted in the capture of Belleau Woods after very severe fighting. The village of Bouresches was taken soon after, and on July 1 Vaux was captured. In these operations the Second Division met with most desperate resistance by Germany's best troops.

14. To meet the March offensive, the French had extended their front from the Oise to Amiens, about 60 kilometers, and during the German drive along the Lys had also sent reinforcements to assist the British. The French lines had been further lengthened about 45 kilometers as a result of the Marne pocket made by the Aisne offensive. This increased frontage and the heavy fighting had reduced French reserves to an extremely low point.

Our Second Corps, under Maj. Gen. George W. Read, had been organized for the command of the 10 divisions with the British, which were held back in training areas or assigned to second-line defenses. After consultation with Field Marshal Haig on June 3, 5 American divisions were relieved from the British area to support the French. The Seventy-seventh and Eighty-second Divisions were moved south to release the Forty-second and Twenty-sixth for employment on a more active portion of the front; the Thirty-fifth Division entered the line in the Vosges, and the Fourth and Twenty-eighth Divisions were moved to the region of Meaux and Chateau-Thierry as reserves.

MEN OF THE 28TH INF. IN THE MONTDIDIER SECTOR

On June 9 the Germans attacked the Montdidier-Noyon front in an effort to widen the Marne pocket and bring their lines nearer to Paris, but were stubbornly held by the French with comparatively little loss of ground. In view of the unexpected results of the three preceding attacks by the enemy, this successful defense proved beneficial to the Allied morale, particularly as it was believed that the German losses were unusually heavy.

15. On July 15, the date of the last German offensive, the First, Second, Third, and Twenty-sixth Divisions were on the Chateau-Thierry front with the Fourth and Twenty-eighth in support, some small units of the last two divisions gaining front-line experience with our troops or with the French; the Forty-second Division was in support of the French east of Rheims; and four colored regiments were with the French in the Argonne. On the Alsace-Lorraine front we had five divisions in line with the French. Five were with the British Army, three having elements in the line. In our training areas four divisions were assembled and four were in the process of arrival.

The Marne salient was inherently weak and offered an opportunity for a counteroffensive that was obvious. If successful, such an operation would afford immediate relief to the Allied defense, would remove the threat against Paris, and free the Paris-Nancy Railroad. But, more important than all else, it would restore the morale of the Allies and remove the profound depression and fear then existing. Up to this time our units had been put in here and there at critical points as emergency troops to stop the terrific German advance. In every trial, whether on the defensive or offensive, they had proved themselves equal to any troops in Europe. As early as June 23 and again on July 10 at Bombon, I had very strongly urged that our best divisions be concentrated under American command, if possible, for use as a striking force against the Marne salient. Although the prevailing view among the Allies was that American units were suitable only for the defensive, and that at all events they could be used to better advantage under Allied command, the suggestion was accepted in principle, and my estimate of their offensive fighting qualities was soon put to the test.

The enemy had encouraged his soldiers to believe that the July 15 attack would conclude the war with a German peace. Although he made elaborate plans for the operation, he failed to conceal fully his intentions, and the front of attack was suspected at least one week ahead. On the Champagne front the actual hour for the assault was known and the enemy was checked with heavy losses. The Forty-second Division entered the line near Somme Py immediately, and five of its infantry battalions and all its artillery became engaged. Southwest of Rheims and along the Marne to the east of Chateau-Thierry the Germans were at first somewhat successful, a penetration of 8 kilometers beyond the river being effected against the French immediately to the right of our Third Division. The following quotation from the report of the commanding general Third Division gives the result of the fighting on his front:

"Although the rush of the German troops overwhelmed some of the front-line positions, causing the infantry and machine-gun companies to suffer, in some cases a 50 per cent loss, no German soldier crossed the road from Fossoy to Crezancy, except as a prisoner of war, and by noon of the following day (July 16) there were no Germans in the foreground of the Third Division sector except the dead."

On this occasion a single regiment of the Third Division wrote one of the most brilliant pages in our military annals. It prevented the crossing at certain points on its front, while on either flank the Germans who had gained a footing pressed forward. Our men, firing in three directions, met the German attacks with counterattacks at critical points and succeeded in throwing two German divisions into complete confusion, capturing 600 prisoners.

16. The selection by the Germans of the Champagne sector and the eastern and southern faces of the Marne pocket on which to make their offensive was fortunate for the Allies, as it favored the launching of the counterattack already planned. There were now over 1,200,000 American troops in France, which provided a considerable force of reserves. Every American division with any sort of training was made available for use in a counteroffensive.

Gen. Petain's initial plan for the counterattack involved the entire western face of the Marne salient. The First and Second American Divisions, with the First French Moroccan Division between them, were employed as the spearhead of the main attack, driving directly eastward, through the most sensitive portion of the German lines, to the heights south of Soissons. The advance began on July 18, without the usual brief warning of a preliminary bombardment, and these three divisions at a single bound broke through the enemy's infantry defenses and overran his artillery, cutting or interrupting the German communications leading into the salient. A general withdrawal from the Marne was immediately begun by the enemy, who still fought stubbornly to prevent disaster.

The First Division, throughout 4 days of constant fighting, advanced 11 kilometers, capturing Berzy-le-Sec and the heights above Soissons and taking some 3,500 prisoners and 68 field guns from the 7 German divisions employed against it. It was relieved by a British division. The Second Division advanced 8 kilometers in the first 26 hours, and by the end of the second day was facing Tigny, having captured 3,000 prisoners and 66 field guns. It was relieved the night of the 19th by a French division. The result of this counteroffensive was

of decisive importance. Due to the magnificent dash and power displayed on the field of Soissons by our First and Second Divisions the tide of war was definitely turned in favor of the Allies.

Other American divisions participated in the Marne counteroffensive. A little to the south of the Second Division, the Fourth was in line with the French and was engaged until July 22. The First American Corps, Maj. Gen. Hunter Liggett commanding, with the Twenty-sixth Division and a French division, acted as a pivot of the movement toward Soissons, capturing Torcy on the 18th and reaching the Chateau-Thierry-Soissons road on the 21st. At the same time the Third Division crossed the Marne and took the heights of Mont St. Pere and the villages of Charteves and Jaulgonne.

In the First Corps, the Forty-second Division relieved the Twenty-sixth on July 25 and extended its front, on the 26th relieving the French division. From this time until August 2 it fought its way through the Forest de Fere and across the Ourcq, advancing toward the Vesle until relieved by the Fourth Division on August 3. Early in this period elements of the Twenty-eighth Division participated in the advance.

Farther to the east the Third Division forced the enemy back to Roncheres Wood, where it was relieved on July 30 by the Thirty-second Division from the Vosges front. The Thirty-second, after relieving the Third and some elements of the Twenty-eighth on the line of the Ourcq River, advanced abreast of the Forty-second toward the Vesle. On August 3 it passed under control of our Third Corps, Maj. Gen. Robert L. Bullard commanding, which made its first appearance in battle at this time, while the Fourth Division took up the task of the Forty-second Division and advanced with the Thirty-second to the Vesle River, where, on August 6, the operation for the reduction of the Marne salient terminated.

In the hard fighting from July 18 to August 6 the Germans were not only halted in their advance but were driven back from the Marne

STEMMING THE TIDE AT CHATEAU-THIERRY. 3RD DIVISION TROOPS GUARDING THE BRIDGEHEAD AT CHATEAU-THIERRY.

15499

AGAINST PASSAGE OF THE MARNE BY THE GERMANS

to the Vesle and committed wholly to the defensive. The force of American arms had been brought to bear in time to enable the last offensive of the enemy to be crushed.

17. The First and Third Corps now held a continuous front of 11 kilometers along the Vesle. On August 12 the Seventy-seventh Division relieved the Fourth Division on the First Corps front, and the following day the Twenty-eighth relieved the Thirty-second Division in the Third Corps, while from August 6 to August 10 the Sixth Infantry Brigade of the Third Division held a sector on the river line. The transfer of the First Corps to the Woevre was ordered at this time, and the control of its front was turned over to the Third Corps.

On August 18 Gen. Petain began an offensive between Rheims and the Oise. Our Third Corps participated in this operation, crossing the Vesle on September 4 with the Twenty-eighth and Seventy-seventh Divisions and overcoming stubborn opposition on the plateau south of the Aisne, which was reached by the Seventy-seventh on September 6. The Twenty-eighth was withdrawn from the line on September 7. Two days later the Third Corps was transferred to the region of Verdun, the Seventy-seventh Division remaining in line on the Aisne River until September 17.

The Thirty-second Division, upon its relief from the battle on the Vesle, joined a French corps north of Soissons and attacked from August 29 to 31, capturing Juvigny after some particularly desperate fighting and reaching the Chauny-Soissons road.

18. On the British front two regiments of the Thirty-third Division participated in an attack on Hamel July 4, and again on August 9 as an incident of the allied offensive against the Amiens salient. One of these regiments took Gressaire Wood and Chipilly Ridge, capturing 700 prisoners and considerable matériel.

ASSEMBLING THE FIRST AMERICAN ARMY

19. In conference with Gen. Petain at Chantilly on May 19 it had been agreed that the American Army would soon take complete charge of the sector of the Woevre. The Twenty-sixth Division was already in line in the Woevre north of Toul and was to be followed

THE FINAL ALLIED OFFENSIVE OF 1918
The numbers refer to the American divisions engaged during the offensive.

by other American divisions as they became available, with the understanding that the sector was to pass to our control when four divisions were in the line. But demands of the battle then going on farther west required the presence of our troops, and the agreement had no immediate result. Due to the presence of a number of our divisions northeast of Paris, the organization of an American corps sector in the Chateau-Thierry region was taken up with Gen. Petain, and on July 4 the First Corps assumed tactical control of a sector in that region. This was an important step, but it was by no means satisfactory, as only one American division at the moment was operating under the control of the First Corps, while he had at this time eight American divisions in the front line serving in French corps.

20. The counter-offensives against the Marne salient in July, and against the Amiens salient in August, had gained such an advantage that it was apparent that the emergency, which justified the dispersion of our divisions, had passed. The moment was propitious for assembling our divisions. Scattered as they were along the Allied front, their supply had become very difficult. From every point of view the immediate organization of an independent American force was indicated. The formation of the Army in the Chateau-Thierry region and its early transfer to the sector of the Woevre, which was to extend from Nomeny, east of the Moselle, to north of St. Mihiel, was therefore decided upon by Marshal Foch and myself on August 9, and the details were arranged with Gen. Petain later on the same day.

The St. Mihiel Salient

21. At Bombon on July 24 there was a conference of all the Commanders-in-Chief for the purpose of considering Allied operations. Each presented proposals for the employment of the armies under his command and these formed the basis of future conference of the Allies. It was emphatically determined that the Allied attitude should be to maintain the offensive. As the first operation of the American Army, the reduction of the salient of St. Mihiel was to be undertaken as soon as the necessary troops and material could be made available. On account of the swampy nature of the country it was especially important that the movement be undertaken and finished before the fall rains should begin, which was usually about the middle of September.

Arrangements were concluded for successive relief of American divisions and the organization of the First American Army under my personal command was announced on August 10, with La Ferte-sous-Jouarre as headquarters. This Army nominally assumed control of a portion of the Vesle front, although at the same time directions were given for its secret concentration in the St. Mihiel sector.

22. The force of American soldiers in France at that moment was sufficient to carry out this offensive, but they were dispersed along the front from Switzerland to the Channel. The three Army Corps headquarters to participate in the St. Mihiel attack were the First, Fourth, and Fifth. The First was on the Vesle, the Fourth at Toul, and the Fifth not yet completely organized. To assemble combat divisions and service troops and undertake a major operation, within the short period available and with staffs so recently organized, was an extremely difficult task. Our deficiencies in artillery, aviation, and special troops, caused by the shipment of an undue proportion of infantry and machine guns during the summer, were largely met by the French.

23. The reduction of the St. Mihiel salient was important, as it would prevent the enemy from interrupting traffic on the Paris-Nancy Railroad by artillery fire and would free the railroad leading north through St. Mihiel to Verdun. It would also provide us with an advantageous base of departure for an attack against the Metz-Sedan Railroad system which was vital to the German armies west of Verdun, and against the Briey Iron Basin which was necessary for the production of German armament and munitions.

The general plan was to make simultaneous attacks against the flanks of the salient. The ultimate objective was tentatively fixed as the general line Marieulles (east of the Moselle)—heights south of Gorze-Mars la Tour-Etain. The operation contemplated the use on the western face of 3 or 4 American divisions, supported by the attack of 6 divisions of the Second French Army on their left, while 7 American divisions would attack on the southern face, and 3 French divisions would press the enemy at the tip of the salient. As the part to be taken by the Second French Army would be closely related to the attack of the First American Army, Gen. Petain placed all the French troops involved under my personal command.

By August 30, the concentration of the scattered divisions, corps, and army troops, of the quantities of supplies and munitions required, and the necessary construction of light railways and roads, were well under way.

24. In accordance with the previous general consideration of operations at Bombon on July 24, an allied offensive extending practically along the entire active front was eventually to be carried out. After the reduction of the St. Mihiel sector the Americans were to cooperate in the concerted effort of the Allied armies. It was the sense of the conference of July 24, that the extent to which the different operations already planned might carry us could not be then foreseen, especially if the results expected were achieved before the season was far advanced. It seemed reasonable at that time to look forward to a combined offensive for the autumn, which would give no respite to the enemy and would increase our advantage for the inauguration of succeeding operations extending into 1919.

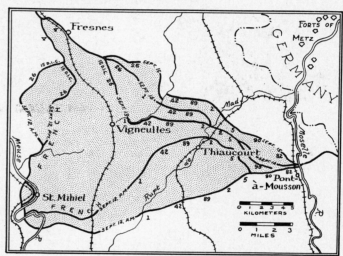

THE ST. MIHIEL DRIVE

On August 30, a further discussion with Marshal Foch was held at my headquarters at Ligny-en-Barrois. In view of the new successes of the French and British near Amiens and the continued favorable results toward the Chemin des Dames on the French front, it was now believed that the limited Allied offensive, which was to prepare for the campaign of 1919, might be carried further before the end of the year. At this meeting it was proposed by Marshal Foch that the general operations as far as the American Army was concerned should be carried out in detail by:

(a) An attack between the Meuse and the Argonne by the Second French Army, reinforced by from four to six American divisions.

(b) A French-American attack, extending from the Argonne west to the Souain Road, to be executed on the right by an American Army astride the Aisne and on the left by the Fourth French Army.

To carry out these attacks the 10 to 11 American divisions suggested for the St. Mihiel operation and the 4 to 6 for the Second French Army, would leave 8 to 10 divisions for an American Army on the Aisne. It was proposed that the St. Mihiel operation should be initiated on September 10 and the other two on September 15 and 20, respectively.

"I HAVE A RENDEZVOUS WITH DEATH"

25. The plan suggested for the American participation in these operations was not acceptable to me because it would require the immediate separation of the recently formed First American Army into several groups, mainly to assist French armies. This was directly contrary to the principle of forming a distinct American Army, for which my contention had been insistent. An enormous amount of preparation had already been made in construction of roads, railroads, regulating stations, and other installations looking to the use and supply of our armies on a particular front. The inherent disinclination of our troops to serve under allied commanders would have grown and American morale would have suffered. My position was stated quite clearly that the strategical employment of the First Army as a unit would be undertaken where desired, but its disruption to carry out these proposals would not be entertained.

A further conference at Marshal Foch's headquarters was held on September 2, at which Gen. Petain was present. After discussion the question of employing the American Army as a unit was conceded. The essentials of the strategical decision previously arrived at provided that the advantageous situation of the Allies should be exploited to the utmost by vigorously continuing the general battle and extending it eastward to the Meuse. All the Allied armies were to be employed in a converging action. The British armies, supported by the left of the French armies, were to pursue the attack in the direction of Cambrai; the center of the French armies, west of Rheims, would continue the actions, already begun, to drive the enemy beyond the Aisne; and the American Army, supported by the right of the French armies, would direct its attack on Sedan and Mezieres.

It should be recorded that although this general offensive was fully outlined at the conference no one present expressed the opinion that the final victory could be won in 1918. In fact, it was believed by the French high command that the Meuse-Argonne attack could not be pushed much beyond Montfaucon before the arrival of winter would force a cessation of operations.

26. The choice between the two sectors, that east of the Aisne including the Argonne Forest, or the Champagne sector, was left to me. In my opinion, no other Allied troops had the morale or the offensive spirit to overcome successfully the difficulties to be met in the Meuse-Argonne sector and our plans and installations had been prepared for an expansion of operations in that direction. So the Meuse-Argonne front was chosen. The entire sector of 150 kilometers of front, extending from Port-sur-Seille, east of the Moselle, west to include the Argonne Forest, was accordingly placed under my command, including all French divisions then in that zone. The First American Army was to proceed with the St. Mihiel operation, after which the operation between the Meuse and the western edge of the Argonne Forest was to be prepared and launched not later than September 25.

As a result of these decisions, the depth of the St. Mihiel operation was limited to the line Vigneulles-Thiaucourt-Regnieville. The number of divisions to be used was reduced and the time shortened. Eighteen to 19 divisions were to be in the front line. There were 4 French and 15 American divisions available, 6 of which would be in reserve, while the two flank divisions of the front line were not to advance. Furthermore, 2 Army Corps headquarters, with their corps troops, practically all the Army artillery and aviation, and the First, Second, and Fourth Divisions, the first two destined to take a leading part in the St. Mihiel attack, were all due to be withdrawn and started for the Meuse-Argonne by the fourth day of the battle.

27. The salient had been held by the Germans since September, 1914. It covered the most sensitive section of the enemy's position on the Western Front; namely, the Mezieres-Sedan-Metz Railroad and the Briey-Iron Basin; it threatened the entire region between Verdun and Nancy, and interrupted the main rail line from Paris to the east. Its primary strength lay in the natural defensive features of the terrain itself. The western face of the salient extended along the rugged, heavily wooded eastern heights of the Meuse; the southern face followed the heights of the Meuse for 8 kilometers to the east and then crossed the plain of the Woevre, including within the German lines the detached heights of Loupmont and Montsec which dominated the plain

and afforded the enemy unusual facilities for observation. The enemy had reinforced the positions by every artificial means during a period of four years.

28. On the night of September 11, the troops of the First Army were deployed in position. On the southern face of the salient was the First Corps, Maj. Gen. Liggett, commanding, with the Eighty-second, Ninetieth, Fifth, and Second Divisions in line, extending from the Moselle westward. On its left was the Fourth Corps, Maj. Gen. Joseph T. Dickman, commanding, with the Eighty-ninth, Forty-second, and First Divisions, the left of this corps being opposite Montsec. These two Army Corps were to deliver the principal attack, the line pivoting on the center division of the First Corps. The First Division on the left of the Fourth Corps was charged with the double mission of covering its own flank while advancing some 20 kilometers due north toward the heart of the salient, where it was to make contact with the troops of the Fifth Corps. On the western face of the salient lay the Fifth Corps, Maj. Gen. George H. Cameron, commanding, with the Twenty-sixth Division, Fifteenth French Colonial Division, and the Fourth Division in line, from Mouilly west to Les Eparges and north to Watronville. Of these three divisions, the Twenty-sixth alone was to make a deep advance directed southeast toward Vigneulles. The French Division was to make a short progression to the edge of the heights in order to cover the left of the Twenty-sixth. The Fourth Division was not to advance. In the center, between our Fourth and Fifth Army Corps, was the Second French Colonial Corps, Maj. Gen. E. J. Blondlat, commanding, covering a front of 40 kilometers with 3 small French divisions. These troops were to follow up the retirement of the enemy from the tip of the salient.

The French independent air force was at my disposal which, together with the British bombing squadrons and our own air forces, gave us the largest assembly of aviation that had ever been engaged in one operation. Our heavy guns were able to reach Metz and to interfere seriously with German rail movements.

At dawn on September 12, after four hours of violent artillery fire of preparation, and accompanied by small tanks, the infantry of the First and Fourth Corps advanced. The infantry of the Fifth Corps commenced its advance at 8 a. m. The operation was carried out with entire precision. Just after daylight on September 13, elements of the First and Twenty-sixth Divisions made a junction near Hattonchatel and Vigneulles, 18 kilometers northeast of St. Mihiel. The rapidity with which our divisions advanced overwhelmed the enemy, and all objectives were reached by the afternoon of September 13. The enemy had apparently started to withdraw some of his troops from the tip of the salient on the eve of our attack, but had been unable to carry it through. We captured nearly 16,000 prisoners, 443 guns, and large stores of material and supplies. The energy and swiftness with which the operation was carried out enabled us to smother opposition to such an extent that we suffered less than 7,000 casualties during the actual period of the advance.

During the next two days the right of our line west of the Moselle River was advanced beyond the objectives laid down in the original orders. This completed the operation for the time being and the line was stabilized to be held by the smallest practical force.

29. The material results of the victory achieved were very important. An American Army was an established fact, and the enemy had felt its power. No form of propaganda could overcome the depressing effect on the morale of the enemy of this demonstration of our ability to organize a large American force and drive it successfully through his defenses. It gave our troops implicit confidence in their superiority and raised their morale to the highest pitch. For the first time wire entanglements ceased to be regarded as impassable barriers and open-warfare training, which had been so urgently insisted upon, proved to be the correct doctrine. Our divisions concluded the attack with such small losses and in such high spirits that without the usual rest they were immediately available for employment in heavy fighting in a new theater of operations. The strength of the First Army in this battle totaled approximately 500,000 men, of whom about 70,000 were French.

"AT SOME DISPUTED BARRICADE"

The Meuse-Argonne Front

30. The definite decision for the Meuse-Argonne phase of the great allied convergent attack was agreed to in my conference with Marshal Foch and Gen. Petain on September 2. It was planned to use all available forces of the First Army, including such divisions and troops as we might be able to withdraw from the St. Mihiel front. The Army was to break through the enemy's successive fortified zones to include the Kriemhilde-Stellung, or Hindenburg Line, on the front Brieulles-Romagne sous Montfaucon-Grandpre, and thereafter, by developing pressure toward Mezieres, was to insure the fall of the Hindenburg Line along the Aisne River in front of the Fourth French Army, which was to attack to the west of the Argonne Forest. A penetration of some 12 to 15 kilometers was required to reach the Hindenburg Line on our front, and the enemy's defenses were virtually continuous throughout that depth.

The Meuse-Argonne front had been practically stabilized in September, 1914, and, except for minor fluctuations during the German attacks on Verdun in 1916 and the French counteroffensive in August, 1917, remained unchanged until the American advance in 1918. The net result of the four years' struggle on this ground was a German defensive system of unusual depth and strength and a wide zone of utter devastation, itself a serious obstacle to offensive operations.

31. The strategical importance of this portion of the line was second to none on the western front. All supplies and evacuations of the German Armies in northern France were dependent upon two great railway systems—one in the north, passing through Liege, while the other in the south, with lines coming from Luxemburg, Thionville, and Metz, had as its vital section the line Carignan-Sedan-Mezieres. No other important lines were available to the enemy, as the mountainous masses of the Ardennes made the construction of east and west lines through that region impracticable. The Carignan-Sedan-Mezieres line

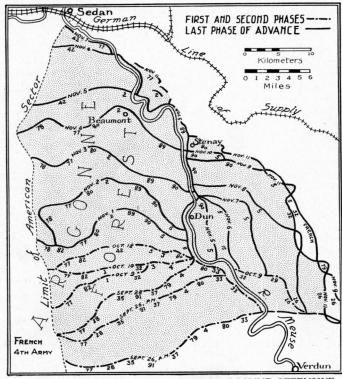

AMERICAN DIVISIONS IN THE MEUSE-ARGONNE OFFENSIVE

was essential to the Germans for the rapid strategical movement of troops. Should this southern system be cut by the Allies before the enemy could withdraw his forces through the narrow neck between Mezieres and the Dutch frontier, the ruin of his armies in France and Belgium would be complete.

From the Meuse-Argonne front the perpendicular distance to the Carignan-Mezieres railroad was 50 kilometers. This region formed the pivot of German operations in northern France, and the vital necessity of covering the great railroad line into Sedan resulted in the convergence on the Meuse-Argonne front of the successive German defensive position. It will be seen, for example, that the distance between "no man's land" and the third German withdrawal position in the vicinity of the Meuse River was approximately 18 kilometers; the distance between the corresponding points near the tip of the great salient of the western front was about 65 kilometers, and in the vicinity of Cambrai was over 30 kilometers. The effect of a penetration of 18 kilometers by the American Army would be equivalent to an advance of 65 kilometers farther west; furthermore, such an advance on our front was far more dangerous to the enemy than an advance elsewhere. The vital importance of this portion of his position was fully appreciated by the enemy, who had suffered tremendous losses in 1916 in attempting to improve it by the reduction of Verdun. As a consequence it had been elaborately fortified, and consisted of practically a continuous series of positions 20 kilometers or more in depth.

In addition to the artificial defenses, the enemy was greatly aided by the natural features of the terrain. East of the Meuse the dominating heights not only protected his left but gave him positions from which powerful artillery could deliver an oblique fire on the western bank. Batteries located in the elaborately fortified Argonne forest covered his right flank, and could cross their fire with that of the guns on the east bank of the Meuse. Midway between the Meuse and

the forest the heights of Montfaucon offered perfect observation and formed a strong natural position which had been heavily fortified. The east and west ridges abutting on the Meuse and Aire River valleys afforded the enemy excellent machine-gun positions for the desperate defense which the importance of the position would require him to make. North of Montfaucon densely wooded and rugged heights constituted natural features favorable to defensive fighting.

32. When The First Army became engaged in the simultaneous preparation for two major operations, an interval of 14 days separated the initiation of the two attacks. During this short period of the movement of the immense number of troops and the amount of supplies involved in the Meuse-Argonne battle, over the few roads available, and confined entirely to the hours of darkness, was one of the most delicate and difficult problems of the war. The concentration included 15 divisions of which 7 were involved in the pending St. Mihiel drive, 3 were in sector in the Vosges, 3 in the neighborhood of Soissons, 1 in a training area, and 1 near Bar-le-Duc. Practically all the artillery, aviation, and other auxiliaries to be employed in the new operations were committed to the St. Mihiel attack and therefore could not be moved until its success was assured. The concentration of all units not to be used at St. Mihiel was commenced immediately, and on September 13, the second day of St. Mihiel, reserve divisions and Army Artillery units were withdrawn and placed in motion toward the Argonne front.

That part of the American sector from Fresnes-en-Woevre, southeast of Verdun, to the western edge of the Argonne Forest, while nominally under my control, did not actively become a part of my command until September 22, on which date my headquarters were established at Souilly, southwest of Verdun. Of French troops, in addition to the Second French Colonial Corps, composed of 3 divisions, there was also the Seventeenth French Corps of 3 divisions holding the front north and east of Verdun.

"AT MIDNIGHT IN SOME FLAMING TOWN"

33. At the moment of the opening of the Meuse-Argonne battle, the enemy had 10 divisions in line and 10 in reserve on the front between Fresnes-en-Woevre and the Argonne Forest, inclusive. He had undoubtedly expected a continuation of our advance toward Metz. Successful ruses were carried out between the Meuse River and Luneville to deceive him as to our intentions, and French troops were maintained as a screen along our front until the night before the battle, so that the actual attack was a tactical surprise.

34. The operations in the Meuse-Argonne battle really form a continuous whole, but they extended over such a long period of continuous fighting that they will be considered in three phases, the first from September 26 to October 3, the second from October 4 to 31, and the third from November 1 to 11.

35. On the night of September 25, the 9 divisions to lead in the attack were deployed between the Meuse River and the western edge of the Argonne Forest. On the right was the Third Corps, Maj. Gen. Bullard commanding, with the Thirty-third, Eightieth, and Fourth Divisions in line; next came the Fifth Corps, Maj. Gen. Cameron commanding, with the Seventy-ninth, Thirty-seventh, and Ninety-first Divisions; on the left was the First Corps, Maj. Gen. Liggett commanding, with the Thirty-fifth, Twenty-eighth, and Seventy-seventh Divisions. Each corps had 1 division in reserve and the Army held 3 divisions as a general reserve. About 2,700 guns,

189 small tanks, 142 manned by Americans, and 821 airplanes, 604 manned by Americans, were concentrated to support the attack of the infantry. We thus had a superiority in guns and aviation, and the enemy had no tanks.

The axis of the attack was the line Montfaucon-Romagne-Buzancy, the purpose being to make the deepest penetration in the center, which, with the Fourth French Army advancing west of the Argonne, would force the enemy to evacuate that forest without our having to deliver a heavy attack in that difficult region.

36. Following three hours of violent artillery fire of preparation, the infantry advanced at 5:30 a. m. on September 26, accompanied by tanks. During the first two days of the attack, before the enemy was able to bring up his reserves, our troops made steady progress through the network of defenses. Montfaucon was held tenaciously by the enemy and was not captured until noon of the second day.

By the evening of the 28th a maximum advance of 11 kilometers had been achieved and we had captured Baulny, Epinonville, Septsarges, and Dannevoux. The right had made a splendid advance into the woods south of Brieulles-sur-Meuse, but the extreme left was meeting strong resistance in the Argonne. The attack continued without interruption, meeting six new divisions which the enemy threw into the first line before September 29. He developed a powerful machine gun defense supported by heavy artillery fire, and made

"AND I TO MY PLEDGED WORD AM TRUE, I SHALL NOT FAIL THAT RENDEZVOUS"

frequent counter-attacks with fresh troops, particularly on the front of the Twenty-eighth and Thirty-fifth Divisions. These divisions had taken Varennes, Cheppy, Baulny, and Charpentry, and the line was within 2 kilometers of Apremont. We were no longer engaged in a maneuver for the pinching out of a salient, but were necessarily committed, generally speaking, to a direct frontal attack against strong, hostile positions fully manned by a determined enemy.

37. By nightfall of the 29th the First Army line was approximately Bois de la Cote Lemont—Nantillois—Apremont—southwest across the Argonne. Many divisions, especially those in the center that were subjected to cross-fire of artillery, had suffered heavily. The severe fighting, the nature of the terrain over which they attacked, and the fog and darkness sorely tried even our best divisions. On the night of the 29th the Thirty-seventh and Seventy-ninth Divisions were relieved by the Thirty-second and Third Divisions, respectively, and on the following night the First Division relieved the Thirty-fifth Division.

38. The critical problem during the first few days of the battle was the restoration of communications over "no man's land." There were but four roads available across this deep zone, and the violent artillery fire of the previous period of the war had virtually destroyed them. The spongy soil and the lack of material increased the difficulty. But the splendid work of our engineers and pioneers soon made possible the movement of the troops, artillery, and supplies most needed. By the afternoon of the 27th all the divisional artillery, except a few batteries of heavy guns, had effected a passage and was supporting the infantry action.

MEUSE-ARGONNE, SECOND PHASE

39. At 5:30 a. m. on October 4 the general attack was renewed. The enemy divisions on the front from Fresnes-en-Woevre to the Argonne had increased from 10 in first line to 16, and included some of his best divisions. The fighting was desperate, and only small advances were realized, except by the First Division on the right of the First Corps. By evening of October 5 the line was approximately Bois de la Cote Lemont-Bois du Fays-Gesnes-Hill 240-Fleville-Chehery, southwest through the Argonne.

It was especially desirable to drive the enemy from his commanding positions on the heights east of the Meuse, but it was even more important that we should force him to use his troops there and weaken his tenacious hold on positions in our immediate front. The further stabilization of the new St. Mihiel line permitted the withdrawal of certain divisions for the extension of the Meuse-Argonne operation to the east bank of the Meuse River.

40. On the 7th the First Corps, with the Eighty-second Division added, launched a strong attack northwest toward Cornay, to draw

attention from the movement east of the Meuse and at the same time outflank the German position in the Argonne. The following day the Seventeenth French Corps, Maj. Gen. Claudel commanding, initiated its attack east of the Meuse against the exact point on which the German armies must pivot in order to withdraw from northern France. The troops encountered elaborate fortifications and stubborn resistance, but by nightfall had realized an advance of 6 kilometers to a line well within the Bois de Consenvoye, and including the villages of Beaumont and Haumont. Continuous fighting was maintained along our entire battle front, with especial success on the extreme left, where the capture of the greater part of the Argonne Forest was completed. The enemy contested every foot of ground on our front in order to make more rapid retirements farther west and withdraw his forces from northern France before the interruption of his railroad communications through Sedan.

41. We were confronted at this time by an insufficiency of replacements to build up exhausted divisions. Early in October combat units required some 90,000 replacements, and not more than 45,000 would be available before November 1 to fill the existing and prospective vacancies. We still had two divisions with the British and two with the French. A review of the situation, American and Allied, especially as to our own resources in men for the next two months, convinced me that the attack of the First Army and of the Allied Armies further west should be pushed to the limit. But if the First Army was to continue its aggressive tactics our divisions then with the French must be recalled, and replacements must be obtained by breaking up newly arrived divisions.

In discussing the withdrawal of our divisions from the French with Marshal Foch and Gen. Petain, on October 10, the former expressed his appreciation of the fact that the First Army was striking the pivot of the German withdrawal, and also held the view that the Allied attack should continue. Gen. Petain agreed that the American divisions with the French were essential to us if we were to maintain our battle against the German pivot. The French were, however, straining every nerve to keep up their attacks and, before those divisions with the French had been released, it became necessary for us to send the Thirty-seventh and Ninety-first Divisions from the First Army to assist the Sixth French Army in Flanders.

42. At this time the First Army was holding a front of more than 120 kilometers; its strength exceeded 1,000,000 men; it was engaged in the most desperate battle of our history, and the burden of command was too heavy for a single commander and staff. Therefore, on October 12, that portion of our front extending from Port-sur-Seille, east of the Moselle, to Fresnes-en-Woevre, southeast of Verdun, was transferred to the newly constituted Second Army with Lieut. Gen. Robert L. Bullard in command, under whom it began preparations for the extension of operations to the east in the direction of Briey and Metz. On October 16 the command of the First Army was transferred to Lieut. Gen. Hunter Liggett, and my advance headquarters was established at Ligny-en-Barrois, from which the command of the group of American Armies was exercised.

43. Local attacks of the First Army were continued in order particularly to adjust positions preparatory to a renewed general assault. The First and Fifth Divisions were relieved by the Forty-second and Eightieth Divisions, which were now fresh. An attack along the whole front was made on October 14. The resistance encountered was stubborn, but the stronghold on Cote Dame Marie was captured and the Hindenburg Line was broken. Cunel and Romagne-sous-Montfaucon were taken and the line advanced 2 kilometers north of Sommerance. A maximum advance of 17 kilometers had been made since September 26 and the enemy had been forced to throw into the fight a total of 15 reserve divisions.

During the remainder of the month important local operations were carried out, which involved desperate fighting. The First Corps, Maj. Gen. Dickman commanding, advanced through Grandpre; the Fifth Corps, Maj. Gen. Charles P. Summerall commanding, captured the Bois de Bantheville; the Third Corps, Maj. Gen. John L. Hines commanding, completed the occupation of Cunel Heights; and the Seventeenth French Corps drove the enemy from the main ridge south of La Grande Montagne. Particularly heavy fighting occurred east of

the Meuse on October 18, and in the further penetration of the Kriemhilde-Stellung on October 23 the Twenty-sixth Division entering the battle at this time relieved the Eighteenth French Division.

44. Summarizing the material results which had been attained by the First Army by the end of October, we had met an increasing number of Germany's best divisions, rising from 20 in line and reserve on September 26, to 31 on October 31; the enemy's elaborately prepared positions, including the Hindenburg line, in our front had been broken; the almost impassable Argonne Forest was in our hands; an advance of 21 kilometers had been effected; 18,600 prisoners, 370 cannon, 1,000 machine guns, and a mass of material captured; and the great railway artery through Carignan to Sedan was now seriously threatened.

The demands of incessant battle which had been maintained day by day for more than a month had compelled our divisions to fight to the limit of their capacity. Combat troops were held in line and pushed to the attack until deemed incapable of further effort because of casualties or exhaustion; artillery once engaged was seldom withdrawn and many batteries fought until practically all the animals were casualties and the guns were towed out of line by motor trucks. The American soldier had shown unrivaled fortitude in this continuous fighting during the most inclement weather and under many disadvantages of position. Through experience, the Army had developed into a powerful and smooth-running machine, and there was a supreme confidence in our ability to carry the task successfully.

While the high pressure of these dogged attacks was a great strain on our troops, it was calamitous to the enemy. His divisions had been thrown into confusion by our furious assaults, and his morale had been reduced until his will to resist had well-nigh reached the breaking point. Once a German division was engaged in the fight, it became practically impossible to effect its relief. The enemy was forced to meet the constantly recurring crises by breaking up tactical organizations and sending hurried detachments to widely separated portions of the field.

Every member of the American Expeditionary Forces, from the front line to the base ports, was straining every nerve. Magnificent efforts were exerted by the entire Services of Supply to meet the enormous demands made on it. Obstacles which seemed insurmountable were overcome daily in expediting the movements of replacements, ammunition and supplies to the front, and of sick and wounded to the rear. It was this spirit of determination animating every American soldier that made it impossible for the enemy to maintain the struggle until 1919.

MEUSE-ARGONNE, THIRD PHASE

45. The detailed plans for the operations of the Allied Armies on the western front changed from time to time during the course of this great battle, but the mission of the First American Army to cut the great Carignan-Sedan-Mezieres Railroad remained unchanged. Marshal Foch coordinated the operations along the entire front, continuing persistently and unceasingly the attacks by all Allied Armies; the Belgian Army, with a French Army and two American divisions, advancing eastward; the British Armies and two American divisions, with the First French Army on their right, toward the region north of Givet; the First American Army and Fourth French Army, toward Sedan and Mezieres.

46. On the 21st my instructions were issued to the First Army to prepare thoroughly for a general attack on October 28, that would be decisive if possible. In order that the attack of the First Army and that of the Fourth French Army on its left should be simultaneous, our attack was delayed until November 1. The immediate purpose of the First Army was to take Buzancy and the heights of Barricourt, to turn the forest north of Grandpre, and to establish contact with the Fourth French Army near Boult-aux-Bois. The Army was directed to carry the heights of Barricourt by nightfall of the first day and then to exploit this success by advancing its left to Boult-aux-Bois in preparation for the drive toward Sedan. By strenuous effort all available artillery had been moved well forward to the heights previously occupied by the enemy, from which it could fully cover and support the initial advance of the infantry.

On this occasion and for the first time the Army prepared for its attack under normal conditions. We held the front of attack and were not under the necessity of taking over a new front, with its manifold installations and services. Our own personnel handled the communications, dumps, telegraph lines, and water service; our divisions were either on the line or close in rear; the French artillery, aviation, and technical troops which had previously made up our deficiencies had been largely replaced by our own organizations; and our army, corps, and divisional staffs were by actual experience second to none.

47. On the morning of November 1, three Army corps were in line between the Meuse River and the Bois de Bourgogne. On the right the Third Corps, had the Fifth and Ninetieth Divisions; the Fifth Corps occupied the center of the line, with the Eighty-ninth and Second Divisions, and was to be the wedge of the attack on the first day; and on the left the First Corps deployed the Eightieth, Seventy-seventh, and Seventy-eighth Divisions.

Preceded by two hours of violent artillery preparation, the infantry advanced, closely followed by "accompanying guns." The artillery acquitted itself magnificently, the barrages being so well coordinated and so dense that the enemy was overwhelmed and quickly submerged by the rapid onslaught of the infantry. By nightfall the Fifth Corps, in the center, had realized an advance of almost 9 kilometers, to the Bois de la Folie, and had completed the capture of the heights of Barricourt, while the Third Corps, on the right, had captured Aincreville and Andevanne. Our troops had broken through the enemy's last defense, captured his artillery positions, and had precipitated a retreat of the German forces about to be isolated in the forest north of Grandpre. On the 2d and 3d we advanced rapidly against heavy fighting on the fronts of the right and center corps; to the left the troops of the First Corps hurried forward in pursuit, some by motor trucks, while the artillery pressed along the country roads close behind. Our heavy artillery was skillfully brought into position to fire upon the Carignan-Sedan Railroad and the junction at Longuyon and Conflans. By the evening of the 4th, our troops had reached La Neuville, opposite Stenay, and had swept through the great Foret de Dieulet, reaching the outskirts of Beaumont, while on the left we were 8 kilometers north of Boult-aux-Bois.

The following day the advance continued toward Sedan with increasing swiftness. The Third Corps, turning eastward, crossed the Meuse in a brilliant operation by the Fifth Division, driving the enemy from the heights of Dun-sur-Meuse and forcing a general withdrawal from the strong positions he had so long held on the hills north of Verdun.

By the 7th the right of the Third Corps had exploited its river crossing to a distance of 10 kilometers east of the Meuse, completely ejecting the enemy from the wooded heights and driving him out into the swampy plain of the Woevre; the Fifth and First Corps had reached the line of the Meuse River along their respective fronts and the left of the latter corps held the heights dominating Sedan, the strategical goal of the Meuse-Argonne operation, 41 kilometers from our point of departure on November 1. We had cut the enemy's main line of communications. Recognizing that nothing but a cessation of hostilities could save his armies from complete disaster, he appealed for an immediate armistice on November 6.

48. Meanwhile general plans had been prepared for the further employment of American forces in an advance between the Meuse and the Moselle, to be directed toward Longwy by the First Army, while the Second Army was to assume the offensive toward the Briey Iron Basin. Orders directing the preparatory local operations involved in this enterprise were issued on November 5.

Between the 7th and 10th of November the Third Corps continued its advance eastward to Remoiville, while the Seventeenth French Corps, on its right, with the Seventy-ninth, Twenty-sixth, and Eighty-first American Divisions, and 2 French divisions, drove the enemy from his final foothold on the heights east of the Meuse. At 9 p. m. on November 9 appropriate orders were sent to the First and Second Armies in accordance with the following telegram from Marshal Foch to the Commander of each of the Allied armies:

"The enemy, disorganized by our repeated attacks, retreats along the entire front. It is important to coordinate and expedite our movements. I appeal to the energy and the initiative of the Commanders-in-Chief and of their armies to make decisive the results obtained."

In consequence of the foregoing instructions, our Second Army pressed the enemy along its entire front. On the night of the 10th-11th and the morning of the 11th the Fifth Corps, in the First Army, forced a crossing of the Meuse east of Beaumont and gained the commanding heights within the reentrant of the river, thus completing our control of the Meuse River line. At 6 a. m. on the 11th notification was received from Marshal Foch's headquarters that the Armistice had been signed and that hostilities would cease at 11 a. m. Preparatory measures had already been taken to insure the prompt transmission to the troops of the announcement of an Armistice. However, the advance east of Beaumont on the morning of the 11th had been so rapid and communication across the river was so difficult that there was some fighting on isolated portions of that front after 11 a. m.

49. Between September 26 and November 11, 22 American and 4 French divisions, on the front extending from southeast of Verdun to the Argonne Forest, had engaged and decisively beaten 47 different German divisions, representing 25 per cent of the enemy's entire divisional strength on the western front. Of these enemy divisions 20 had been drawn from the French front and 1 from the British front. Of the 22 American divisions 12 had, at different times during this period, been engaged on fronts other than our own. The First Army suffered a loss of about 117,000 in killed and wounded. It captured 26,000 prisoners, 847 cannon, 3,000 machine guns, and large quantities of material.

The disposition which the enemy made to meet the Meuse-Argonne offensive, both immediately before the opening of the attack and during the battle, demonstrated the importance which he ascribed to this section of the front and the extreme measures he was forced to take in its defense. From the moment the American offensive began until the Armistice, his defense was desperate and the flow of his divisions to our front was continuous.

THE SECOND AMERICAN ARMY

50. Under the instructions issued by me on November 5, for operations by the Second Army in the direction of the Briey Iron Basin, the advance was undertaken along the entire front of the army and continued during the last three days of hostilities. In the face of the stiff resistance offered by the enemy, and with the limited number of troops at the disposal of the Second Army, the gains realized reflected great credit on the divisions concerned. On November 6 Marshal Foch requested that 6 American divisions be held in readiness to assist in an attack which the French were preparing to launch in the direction of Chateau-Salins. The plan was agreed to, but with the provision that our troops should be employed under the direction of the commanding general Second Army.

This combined attack was to be launched on November 14, and was to consist of 20 French divisions under Gen. Mangin and the 6 American divisions under Gen. Bullard. Of the divisions designated for this operation the Third, Fourth, Twenty-ninth, and Thirty-sixth were in Army reserve and were starting their march eastward on the morning of November 11, while the Twenty-eighth and Thirty-fifth were being withdrawn from line on the Second Army front.

AMERICAN ACTIVITIES ON OTHER FRONTS

51. During the first phase of the Meuse-Argonne battle, American divisions were participating in important attacks on other portions of the front. The Second Army Corps, Maj. Gen. Read, commanding, with the Twenty-seventh and Thirtieth Divisions on the British front, was assigned the task in cooperation with the Australian Corps, of breaking the Hindenburg line at Le Cateau, where the St. Quentin Canal passes through a tunnel under a ridge. In this attack, carried out September 29 and October 1, the Thirtieth Division speedily broke through the main line of defense and captured all of its objectives, while the Twenty-seventh progressed until some of its ele-

ments reached Gouy. In this and later actions from October 6 to 19, our Second Corps captured over 6,000 prisoners and advanced about 24 kilometers.

52. On October 2-9 our Second and Thirty-sixth Divisions assisted the Fourth French Army in its advance between Rheims and the Argonne. The Second Division completed its advance on this front by the assault of the wooded heights of Mont Blanc, the key point of the German position, which was captured with consummate dash and skill. The division here repulsed violent counterattacks, and then carried our lines into the village of St. Etienne, thus forcing the Germans to fall back before Rheims and yield positions which they had held since September, 1914. On October 10 the Thirty-sixth Division relieved the Second, exploiting the latter's success, and in two days advanced, with the French, a distance of 21 kilometers, the enemy retiring behind the Aisne River.

53. In the middle of October, while we were heavily engaged in the Meuse-Argonne, Marshal Foch requested that 2 American divisions be sent immediately to assist the Sixth French Army in Belgium, where slow progress was being made. The Thirty-seventh and Ninety-first Divisions, the latter being accompanied by the Artillery of the Twenty-eighth Division, were hurriedly dispatched to the Belgian front. On October 30, in continuation of the Flanders offensive, these divisions entered the line and attacked. By November 3 the Thirty-seventh Division had completed its mission by rapidly driving the enemy across the Escaut River and had firmly established itself on the east bank, while the Ninety-first Division, in a spirited advance, captured Spitaals Bosschen, reached the Scheldt, and entered Audenarde.

AMERICA ON THE ITALIAN FRONT

54. The Italian Government early made request for American troops, but the critical situation on the western front made it neces-

sary to concentrate our efforts there. When the Secretary of War was in Italy during April, 1918, he was urged to send American troops to Italy to show America's interest in the Italian situation and to strengthen Italian morale. Similarly a request was made by the Italian Prime Minister at the Abbeville conference. It was finally

THE ITALIAN FRONT

decided to send one regiment to Italy with the necessary hospital and auxiliary services, and the Three hundred and thirty-second Infantry was selected, reaching the Italian front in July, 1918. These troops participated in action against the Austrians in the fall of 1918 at the crossing of the Piave River and in the final pursuit of the Austrian Army.

MEMBERS OF THE 315TH MACHINE GUN BATTALION ADVANCING THROUGH THE WOOD, 80TH DIVISION, BETWEEN LA CHALADE AND LE CLAON, MEUSE, FRANCE, OCTOBER 29, 1918.

55. It was the opinion of the Supreme War Council that Allied troops should be sent to cooperate with the Russians, either at Murmansk or Archangel, against the Bolshevist forces, and the British Government, through its ambassador at Washington, urged American participation in this undertaking. On July 23, 1918, the War Department directed the dispatch of three battalions of infantry and three companies of engineers to join the Allied expedition. In compliance with these instructions the Three hundred and thirty-ninth Infantry, the First Battalion, Three hundred and tenth Engineers, Three hundred and thirty-seventh Field Hospital Company, and Three hundred and thirty-seventh Ambulance Company were sent through England, whence they sailed on August 26.

The mission of these troops was limited to guarding the ports and as much of the surrounding country as might develop threatening conditions. The Allied force operated under British command, through whose orders the small American contingent was spread over a front of about 450 miles. From September, 1918, to May, 1919, a series of minor engagements with the Bolshevist forces occurred, in which 82 Americans were killed and 7 died of wounds.

In April, 1919, two companies of American railroad troops were added to our contingent. The withdrawal of the American force commenced in the latter part of May, 1919, and on August 25 there was left only a small detachment of Graves Registration troops.

U. S. A. Troops Advance Into Germany

56. In accordance with the terms of the Armistice, the Allies were to occupy all German territory west of the Rhine, with bridgeheads of 30 kilometer radius at Cologne, Coblenz, and Mayence. The zone assigned the American command was the bridgehead of Coblenz and the district of Treves. This territory was to be occupied by an American Army, with its reserves held between the Moselle-Meuse Rivers and the Luxemburg frontier.

The instructions of Marshal Foch, issued on November 16, contemplated that 2 French infantry divisions and 1 French cavalry division would be added to the American forces that occupied the Coblenz bridgehead, and that 1 American division would be added to the French force occupying the Mayence bridgehead. As this arrangement presented possibilities of misunderstanding due to difference of views regarding the government of occupied territory, it was represented to the Marshal that each nation should be given a well-defined territory of occupation, employing within such territory only the troops of the commander responsible for the particular zone. On December 9 Marshal Foch accepted the principle of preserving the entity of command and troops, but reduced the American bridgehead by adding a portion of the eastern half to the French command at Mayence.

57. Various reasons made it undesirable to employ either the First or Second Army as the Army of Occupation. Plans had been made before the Armistice to organize a Third Army and, on November 14, this army, with Maj. Gen. Joseph T. Dickman as commander, was designated as the Army of Occupation. The Third and Fourth Army Corps staffs and troops, less artillery, the First, Second, Third, Fourth, Thirty-second, and Forty-second Divisions, and the Sixty-sixth Field Artillery Brigade were assigned to the Third Army. This force was later increased by the addition of the Seventh Corps, Maj. Gen. William M. Wright commanding, with the Fifth, Eighty-ninth, and Ninetieth Divisions.

The advance toward German territory began on November 17 at 5 a. m., six days after signing the Armistice. All of the Allied forces from the North Sea to the Swiss border moved forward simultaneously in the wake of the retreating German armies. Upon arrival at the frontier, a halt was made until December 1, when the leading elements of all Allied armies crossed the line into Germany. The Third Army Headquarters were established at Coblenz and an Advance General Headquarters located at Treves. Steps were immediately taken to organize the bridgehead for defense, and dispositions were made to meet a possible renewal of hostilities.

The advance to the Rhine required long arduous marches, through cold and inclement weather, with no opportunity for troops to rest, refit, and refresh themselves after their participation in the final battle. The Army of Occupation bore itself splendidly and exhibited a fine state of discipline both during the advance and throughout the period of occupation.

58. The zone of march of our troops into Germany and the line of communications of the Third Army after reaching the Rhine lay through Luxemburg. After the passage of the Third Army, the occupation of Luxemburg, for the purpose of guarding our line of communications, was intrusted to the Fifth and Thirty-third Divisions of the Second Army. The city of Luxemburg, garrisoned by French troops and designated as the headquarters of the Allied Commander-in-Chief, was excluded from our control.

Upon entering the Duchy of Luxemburg in the advance, a policy of noninterference in the affairs of the Grand Duchy was announced. Therefore, when the French commander in the city of Luxemburg was given charge of all troops in the Duchy, in so far as concerned the "administration of the Grand Duchy of Luxemburg," my instructions were that our troops would not be subject to his control. Later, at my request, and in order to avoid possible friction, Marshal Foch placed the entire Duchy in the American Zone.

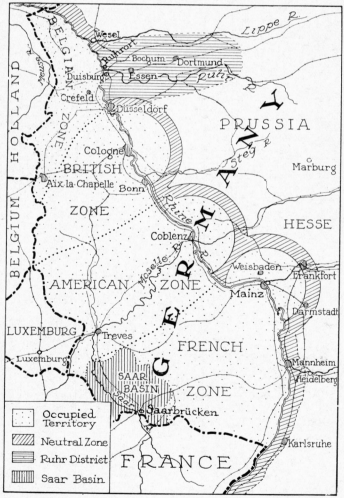

ZONES OF MILITARY OCCUPATION; THE RUHR DISTRICT; AND THE SAAR BASIN

"Here Lie the First Soldiers of the United States to Fall On the Soil of France for Liberty and Justice"

THIS IS THE INSCRIPTION ON THE GRAVES OF CORPORAL JAMES D. GRESHAM AND PRIVATES THOMAS F. ENRIGHT AND MERLE D. HAY OF THE SIXTEENTH INFANTRY, FIRST DIVISION, KILLED ON THE NIGHT OF NOVEMBER 3, 1917, WHEN A GERMAN PATROL RAIDED PART OF THE TRENCHES NEAR BURES OCCUPIED BY AMERICANS.

RETURN OF TROOPS TO THE UNITED STATES

59. On the day the Armistice was signed, the problem of the return of our troops to the United States was taken up with the War Department and, on November 15, a policy recommended of sending home certain auxiliaries so that we could begin to utilize all available shipping without delay. On December 21 the War Department announced by cable that it had been decided to begin immediately the return of our forces and continue as rapidly as transportation would permit. To carry this out, a schedule for the constant flow of troops to the ports was established, having in mind our international obligations pending the signing of the treaty of peace.

60. While more intimately related to the functions of the Services of Supply than to Operations, it is logical to introduce here a brief recital of the organizations created for the return of our troops to America. Prior to the Armistice but 15,000 men had been returned home. Although the existing organization was built for the efficient and rapid handling of the incoming forces, the embarkation of this small number presented no difficulties. But the Armistice suddenly and completely reversed the problem of the Services of Supply at the ports and the handling of troops. It became necessary immediately to reorganize the machinery of the ports, to construct large embarkation camps, and to create an extensive service for embarking the homeward-bound troops.

Brest, St. Nazaire, and Bordeaux became the principal embarkation ports, Marseilles and Le Havre being added later to utilize Italian and French liners. The construction of the embarkation camps during unseasonable winter weather was the most trying problem. These, with the billeting facilities available, gave accommodation for 55,000 at Brest, 44,000 at St. Nazaire, and 130,000 at Bordeaux. Unfortunately, the largest ships had to be handled at Brest, where the least shelter was available.

To maintain a suitable reservoir of men for Brest and St. Nazaire, an Embarkation Center was organized around Le Mans, which eventually accommodated 230,000 men. Here the troops and their records were prepared for the return voyage and immediate demobilization. As the troops arrived at the base ports, the embarkation service was charged with feeding, reclothing, and equipping the hundreds of thousands who passed through, which required the maintenance of a form of hotel service on a scale not hitherto attempted.

61. On November 16 all combat troops, except 30 divisions and a minimum of corps and army troops, were released for return to the United States. It was early evident that only limited use would be made of the American divisions, and that the retention of 30 divisions was not necessary. Marshal Foch considered it indispensable to maintain under arms a total, including Italians, of 120 to 140 divisions, and he proposed that we maintain 30 divisions in France until February 1, 25 of which should be held in the Zone of the Armies, and that on March 1 we should have 20 divisions in the Zone of the Armies and 5 ready to embark. The plan for March 1 was satisfactory, but the restrictions as to the divisions that should be in France on February 1 could not be accepted, as it would seriously interfere with the flow of troops homeward.

In a communication dated December 24 the Marshal set forth the minimum forces to be furnished by the several Allies, requesting the American Army to furnish 22 to 25 divisions of infantry. In the same note he estimated the force to be maintained after the signing of the preliminaries of peace at about 32 divisions, of which the American Army was to furnish 6.

In reply it was pointed out that our problem of repatriation of troops and their demobilization was quite different from that of France or Great Britain. On account of our long line of communications in France and the time consumed by the ocean voyage and travel in the United States, even with the maximum employment of our then available transportation, at least a year must elapse before we could complete our demobilization. Therefore, it was proposed by me that the number of American combat divisions to be maintained in the Zone of the Armies should be reduced on April 1 to 15 divisions and on May 1 to 10 divisions, and that in the unexpected event that the preliminaries of peace should not be signed by May 1 we would continue to maintain 10 divisions in the Zone of the Armies until the date of signature.

The Allied Commander-in-Chief later revised his estimate, and, on January 24, stated to the Supreme War Council that the German demobilization would permit the reduction of the Allied forces to 100 divisions, of which the Americans were requested to furnish 15. In reply, it was again pointed out that our problem was entirely one of transportation, and that such a promise was unnecessary inasmuch as it would probably be the summer of 1919 before we could reduce our forces below the number asked. We were, therefore, able to keep our available ships filled, and by May 19 all combat divisions, except 5 still in the Army of Occupation, were under orders to proceed to ports of embarkation. This provided sufficient troops to utilize all troop transports to include July 15.

62. The President had informed me that it would be necessary for us to have at least one regiment in occupied Germany, and left the details to be discussed by me with Marshal Foch. My cable of July 1 summarizes the agreement reached:

"By direction of President, I have discussed with Marshal Foch question of forces to be left on the Rhine. Following agreed upon: The Fourth and Fifth Divisions will be sent to base ports immediately, the Second Division will commence moving to base ports on July 15, and the Third Division on August 15. Date of relief of First Division will be decided later. Agreement contemplates that after compliance by Germany with military conditions to be completed within first three months after German ratification of treaty, American force will be reduced to one regiment of infantry and certain auxiliaries. Request President be informed of agreement."

As a result of a later conference with Marshal Foch, the Third Division was released on August 3 and the First Division on August 15. I am, Mr. Secretary,

Very Respectfully,

John J. Pershing

General, Commander-in-Chief, American Expeditionary Forces.

GOLD STAR MOTHERS AT GRAVES OF THEIR HONORED SONS IN FRANCE.

"We are the dead; short days ago we lived, felt dawn, saw sunset glow."

"LET'S LOOK AT THE RECORD"

The following summary of America's participation in the World War was compiled from data prepared by Colonel Leonard P. Ayres, Chief of the Statistics Branch of the General Staff. Before becoming a member of the General Staff, Colonel Ayres was director of the Departments of Education and Statistics of the Russell Sage Foundation.

FOUR MILLION MEN

1. The number of men serving in the armed forces of the Nation during the war was 4,800,000, of whom 4,000,000 served in the Army.
2. The British sent more men to France in their first year of war than we did in our first year, but it took England three years to reach a strength of 2,000,000 men in France, and the United States accomplished it in one-half of that time.
3. Of every 100 men who served, 10 were National Guardsmen, 13 were Regulars, and 77 were in the National Army (or would have been if the services had not been consolidated).
4. Of the 54,000,000 males in the population, 26,000,000 were registered in the draft or were already in service.
5. In the physical examinations the States of the Middle West made the best showing. Country boys did better than city boys; whites better than colored; and native born better than foreign born.
6. There were 200,000 Army officers. Of every six officers, one had previous military training with troops, three were graduates of officers' training camps, and two came directly from civil life.

SIX MONTHS OF TRAINING

1. The average American soldier who fought in France had six months of training here, two months overseas before entering the line, and one month in a quiet sector before going into battle.
2. Most soldiers received their training in infantry divisions which are our typical combat units and consist of about 1,000 officers and 27,000 men.
3. Forty-two divisions were sent to France.
4. More than two-thirds of our line officers were graduates of the officers' training camps.
5. France and England sent to the United States nearly 800 specially skilled officers and noncommissioned officers who rendered most important aid as instructors in our training camps.

FOOD, CLOTHING AND EQUIPMENT

1. The problems of feeding and clothing the Army were difficult because of the immense quantities involved rather than because of the difficulty of manufacturing the articles needed.
2. Requirements for some kinds of clothing for the Army were more than twice as great as the prewar total American production of the same articles.
3. To secure the articles needed for the Army the Government had to commandeer all the wool and some other staple articles in the United States and control production through all its stages.
4. The distribution of supplies in the expeditionary forces required the creation of an organization called the Services of Supply, to which one-fourth of all the troops who went overseas were assigned.
5. American Engineers built in France 83 new ship berths, 1,000 miles of standard-gauge track, and 538 miles of narrow-gauge track.
6. The Signal Corps strung in France 100,000 miles of telephone and telegraph wire.
7. Prior to the armistice 40,000 trucks were shipped to the forces in France.
8. Construction projects in the United States cost twice as much as the Panama Canal, and construction overseas was on nearly as large a scale.
9. The Army in France always had enough food and clothing.

SPRINGFIELDS, ENFIELDS AND BROWNINGS

1. The total production of Springfield and Enfield rifles up to the signing of the armistice was over 2,500,000.

2. The use of machine guns on a large scale is a development of the World War. In the American Army the allowance in 1912 was four machine guns per regiment. Army plans now provide for an equipment of 336 guns per regiment, or eighty-four times as many.
3. The entire number of American machine guns produced to the end of 1918 was 227,000.
4. During the war the Browning automatic rifle and the Browning machine gun were developed, put into quantity production, and used in large numbers in the final battles in France.
5. The Browning machine guns are believed to be more effective than the corresponding weapon used in any other army.
6. American production of rifle ammunition amounted to approximately 3,500,000,000, of which 1,500,000,000 were shipped overseas.

TWO THOUSAND GUNS ON THE FIRING LINE

1. When war was declared the United States had sufficient light artillery to equip an army of 500,000 men, and shortly found itself confronted with the problem of preparing to equip 5,000,000 men.
2. To meet the situation it was decided in June, 1917, to allot our guns to training purposes and to equip our forces in France with artillery conforming to the French and British standard calibers.
3. It was arranged that we should purchase from the French and British the artillery needed for our first divisions and ship them in return equivalent amounts of steel, copper, and other raw materials so that they could either manufacture guns for us in their own factories or give us guns out of their stocks and replace them by new ones made from our materials.
4. Up to the end of April, 1919, the number of complete artillery units produced in American plants was more than 3,000, or equal to all those purchased from the French and British during the war.
5. The number of rounds of complete artillery ammunition produced in American plants was in excess of 20,000,000, as compared with 9,000,000 rounds secured from the French and British.

AIRPLANES, MOTORS AND BALLOONS

1. On the declaration of war the United States had 55 training airplanes, of which 51 were classified as obsolete and the other 4 as obsolescent.
2. When we entered the war the Allies made the designs of their planes available to us and before the end of hostilities furnished us from their own manufacture 3,800 service planes.
3. Aviation training schools in the United States graduated 8,602 men from elementary courses and 4,028 from advanced courses. More than 5,000 pilots and observers were sent overseas.
4. The total personnel of the Air Service, officers, students, and enlisted men, increased from 1,200 at the outbreak of the war to nearly 200,000 at its close.
5. There were produced in the United States to November 30, 1918, more than 8,000 training planes and more than 16,000 training engines.
6. The De Haviland-4 observation and day bombing plane was the only plane the United States put into quantity production. Before the signing of the armistice 3,227 had been completed and 1,885 shipped overseas. The plane was successfully used at the front for three months.
7. The production of the 12-cylinder Liberty engine was America's chief contribution to aviation. Before the armistice 13,574 had been completed, 4,435 shipped to the expeditionary forces, and 1,025 delivered to the Allies.

TWO HUNDRED DAYS OF BATTLE

1. Two out of every three American soldiers who reached France took part in battle The number who reached France was 2,084,000 and of these 1,390,000 saw active service at the front.
2. Of the 42 divisions that reached France 29 took part in active combat service. Seven of them were Regular Army divisions, 11

were organized from the National Guard, and 11 were made up of National Army troops.

3. American divisions were in battle for 200 days and engaged in 13 major operations.

4. From the middle of August until the end of the war the American divisions held during the greater part of the time a front longer than that held by the British.

5. In October the American divisions held 101 miles of line, or 23 per cent of the entire western front.

6. On the 1st of April the Germans had a superiority of 324,000 in rifle strength. Due to American arrivals the allied strength exceeded that of the Germans in June and was more than 600,000 above it in November.

7. In the Battle of St. Mihiel 550,000 Americans were engaged, as compared with about 100,000 on the Northern side in the Battle of Gettysburg. The artillery fired more than 1,000,000 shells in four hours, which is the most intense concentration of artillery fire recorded in history.

8. The Meuse-Argonne Battle lasted for 47 days, during which 1,200,000 American troops were engaged.

A MILLION DOLLARS AN HOUR

1. The war cost the United States considerably more than $1,000,000 an hour for over two years.

2. The direct cost was about $32,080,266,968, or nearly enough to pay the entire cost of running the United States Government from 1791 up to the outbreak of the World War.

3. Our expenditures in this war were sufficient to have carried on the Revolutionary War continuously for more than 1,000 years at the rate of expenditure which that war actually involved.

4. In addition to this huge expenditure nearly $10,000,000,000 was loaned by the United States to the Allies.

5. The Army expenditures have been over $14,000,000,000, or nearly two-thirds of our total war costs.

6. During the first three months our war expenditures were at the rate of $2,000,000 per day. During the next year they averaged more than $22,000,000 a day. For the final ten months of the period, the daily average was over $44,000,000.

7. Although the Army expenditures are less than two-thirds of our total war costs, they are nearly equal to the value of all the gold produced in the whole world from the discovery of America up to the outbreak of the World War.

8. The pay of the Army during the war cost more than the combined salaries of all the public-school principals and teachers in the United States for the five years from 1912 to 1916.

9. The total war costs of all nations were about $208,194,860,348, of which the Allies and the United States spent two-thirds and the enemy one-third.

10. The three nations spending the greatest amounts were Germany, Great Britain, and France, in that order. After them come the United States and Austria-Hungary, with substantially equal expenditures.

11. The United States spent about one-eighth of the entire cost of the war, and something less than one-fifth of the expenditures of the Allied side.

WORLD WAR TOLL IN LIVES AND WEALTH

No nation or group of nations was gainer by the World War. The struggle left the original combatants depleted in man-power and wealth, and the best that can be said is that those nations suffered least who were involved least or for the shortest time. There was nothing achieved by any combatant to encourage war as the future policy of any great nation.

CENTRAL POWERS

	Men Mobilized	Dead	Wounded	Prisoners or Missing
Germany	11,000,000	1,773,000	4,216,000	1,152,000
Austria-Hungary	7,800,000	1,200,000	3,620,000	2,200,000
Turkey	2,850,000	325,000	500,000	200,000
Bulgaria	1,200,000	88,000	152,000	28,000
Total	22,850,000	3,386,000	8,488,000	3,580,000

ALLIES

Russia	12,000,000	1,700,000	4,950,000	2,500,000
France	8,410,000	1,358,000	4,266,000	537,000
Britain	8,905,000	908,000	2,090,000	192,000
(Canada)	(595,500)	(64,000)	(150,000)	(3,700)
Italy	5,615,000	650,000	947,000	600,000
Rumania	750,000	335,700	120,000	80,000
United States	4,734,991	130,494	234,000	4,500
Serbia	708,000	45,000	133,000	153,000
Belgium	267,000	14,000	45,000	34,500
Portugal	100,000	7,000	14,000	12,000
Greece	230,000	5,000	21,000	1,000
Montenegro	50,000	3,000	10,000	7,000
Japan	800,000	300	1,000	0
Total	43,165,491	5,220,494	12,831,000	4,121,000

This table is misleading as to weights of forces actually arrayed on either side. Germany's army was comparatively more powerful than the figures show; her men were more fully trained and could be more quickly brought into action than the troops of any other country, and were loyally eager to serve. France equaled Germany in efficiency of troops, but not in numbers and readiness; her eight million "mobilized" represents a more desperate effort than Germany's eleven million. The Austro-Hungarian armies were partly conscripted by force from unwilling subject races, who naturally avoided battle, hence effective Austrian strength was far less than the figures suggest. This was partly true of Turkey also. Russia's enormous numbers were even less efficient; half of them were untrained and half-equipped. British troops were excellent.

As of September 8, 1934, over 100,000 United States World War veterans disabled in service had died; 39,725 were on their backs in hospitals; 9,359 were under domicillary treatment.

DIRECT MONEY COST OF THE WORLD WAR

Computed in part by the United States war department and printed in the Congressional Record, April 14, 1932.

ENTENTE ALLIES

British Empire—	
Great Britain (includes $8,695,000,000 advanced to Allies)	$ 44,029,011,868
Australia	1,437,418,680
Canada	1,665,576,032
India	601,279,000
New Zealand (to Dec. 31, 1918)	378,750,000
Union of South Africa	300,000,000
Belgium	1,154,467,000
France (to Dec. 31, 1918) (includes $1,547,200,000 advanced to Allies)	25,812,782,800
Greece (to Dec. 31, 1918)	270,000,000
Italy (to Oct. 31, 1918)	12,313,998,000
Japan	40,000,000
Rumania	1,600,000,000
Russia (to Dec. 31, 1917)	22,593,950,000
Serbia (now part of Jugoslavia)	399,400,000
United States (includes $9,455,014,125 advanced to Allies)	32,080,266,968
All other Allies (estimated)	500,000,000

CENTRAL POWERS

Germany (includes $2,375,000,000 advanced to allies)	40,150,000,000
Austria-Hungary	20,622,960,000
Bulgaria	815,000,000
Turkey	1,430,000,000
Total	$208,194,860,348

*For detailed account of World War and all events preceding and following the great conflict, consult Progress of Nations (complete 10-volume History of The World) by Jernegan, Benns, Miller and others, published by D. A. V. Dept. of Rehabilitation, 104 South Michigan Ave., Chicago.

· EUROPE IN 1914 ·

· EUROPE AFTER THE WORLD WAR ·

46

OFFICERS IN THE MAKING

When war was declared there were only 6,000 officers in the Regular Army. In officers' training camps it was necessary to crowd a 4 year course into a few months so as to train 180,000 new officers for the National Army.

AMERICA'S GREAT LOTTERY

By June 5, 1917, over 9,500,000 men, between 21 and 31, had registered. Secretary of War Baker, blindfolded, drew the first draft numbers. Not until April, 1918, however, did a National Army division leave for Europe.

TRAINING FOUR MILLION

Before American citizens could be converted into soldiers, they had to be trained in modern warfare. To accomplish this, 16 camps and 16 cantonments, similar to the one pictured above, were constructed in a period of a few months, providing shelter for 1,800,000 men.

SPEEDING PRODUCTION

Major General W. I. Kenly, Commander, Division of Military Aeronautics, addressing the Loyal Legion of Loggers and Lumbermen at a northwest lumber camp where the spruce used in the manufacture of airplanes was obtained.

BUILDING THE AIR FLEET

Less than 25 per cent of the American air squadrons at the front on November 11, 1918 were equipped with American-made machines. The unpreparedness of Uncle Sam was in evidence in every branch of the service.

MANEUVERING THE TANK

The British forces introduced the tank, much to the terror and confusion of the enemy. Here is seen a caterpillar-traction device in action, knocking down a 12-inch tree with the ease that a man's foot crushes a weed.

THE AMERICAN 75 TRACTOR GUN

It looks like an erratic toy but its execution was so deadly that the Germans were willing to give it a lot of ground when it pushed its nose over a trench. Today a tank of this type would be very much out of date.

YOU'RE IN THE ARMY NOW

Bayonet practice at an American army training camp. The men are charging viciously at the swinging dummies. They are being instructed by a British officer who has been "over there" and knows what it is all about.

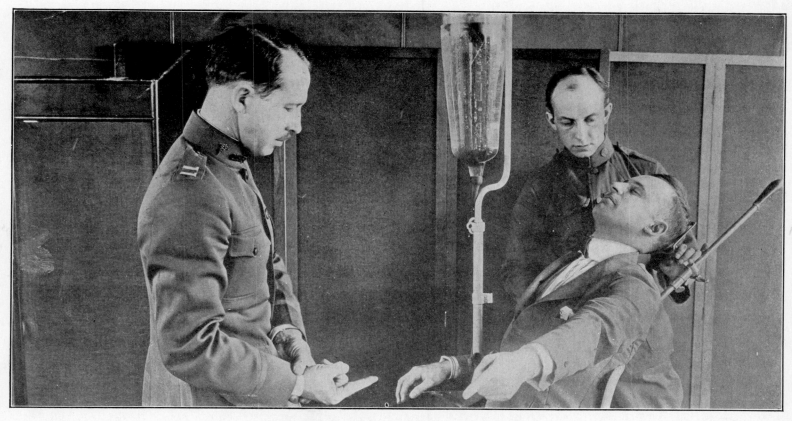

ONLY THE BRAVE DESERVE THE AIR

The man or youth who essayed to be an aviator found the journey to acceptance by the government no easy road. The severity of the tests which applicants were put through was enough to thoroughly discourage the timid.

YOU'RE NOT BEHIND THE PLOW

View at an American military training camp. Men of a training school battery, mounted, drove their guns and caissons through woods, uphill and down and over numerous other obstacles, in order to gain practice in the real life problems that awaited them beyond the Atlantic.

FIRE

American artillerymen training at Camp Zachary Taylor, Louisville, Kentucky. The officer in charge is giving the signal "ready" just as the photographer presses the bulb which exposes the plate in his camera. The gun carriages and shields are painted in camouflage designs.

SCHOOL DAYS

Training candidates in the delicate mechanism of the automatic rifle. In addition to 32 general camps and cantonments, there were schools of training for special services such as Aviation, Artillery, Engineer Corps, Chemical Warfare, Tank Corps and Quartermaster Corps.

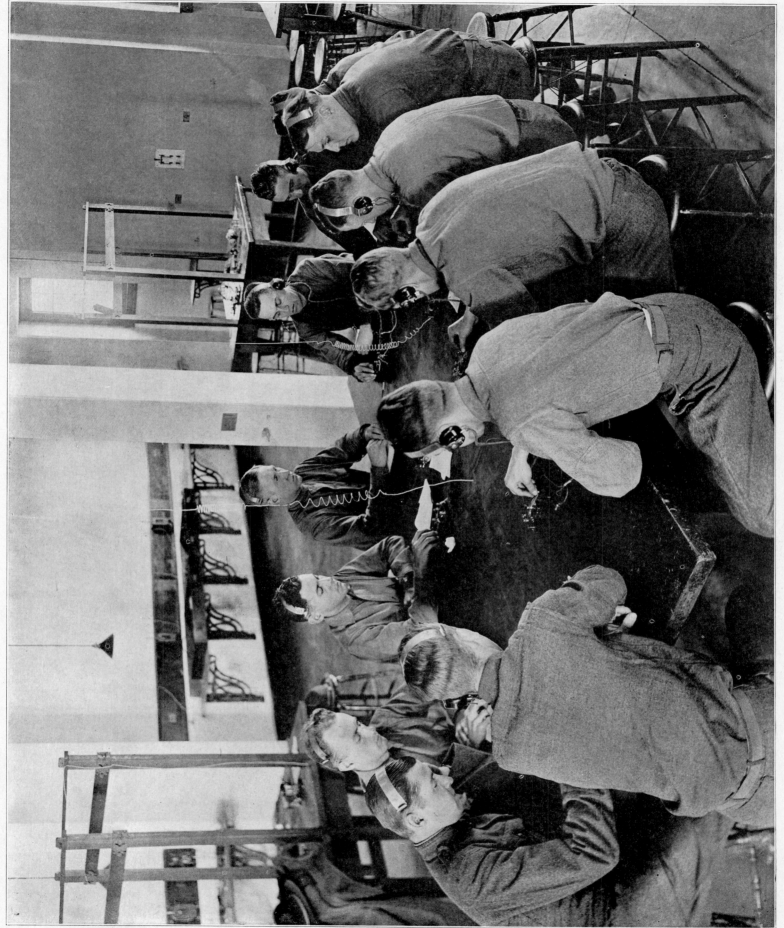

LEARNING THE MORSE CODE

Communications of the army in war were largely dependent upon the Morse code. Telegraph, radio, and the various systems of light, flag and arm signals were dependent upon it. Here is a group of candidates in an officers' school studying the code with the aid of telegraph keys.

FIELD WORK

This photograph shows how war conditions were simulated in training camps. Recruits, practicing the use of a field telegraph set in practice battle fields. However, when our boys reached the front, conditions soon changed. Fighting in the open quickly replaced trench warfare.

LET HER GO

American boys became adept in the use of hand grenades and trench bombs. This is regarded as one of the best explosion photographs ever made.

GOING OVER THE TOP

These new soldiers are shown in a vivid "attack on the enemy" at an American military training camp. Although they are inexperienced in the game, it will be observed that they are putting plenty of pep in the sham charge.

GAS

A charge to Victory through gas-laden air. Soldiers, with gas masks donned, are charging through a hail of exploding gas bombs toward "enemy trenches." With constant false alarms, "gas jitters" became common at the front.

ONE—TWO—THREE—FOUR

Training the Army of the U. S. A. Our boys underwent a well-balanced course of physical training. When this photograph was taken at Camp Hancock, Ga., there were 10,000 of them going through their setting-up exercises.

WHOA

Wooden horses used for preliminary training at a cavalry camp in the United States. These horses, of course, were not to be used as was the wooden horse in the siege of Troy. Uncle Sam had a shortage of real horses.

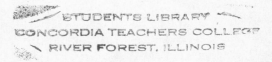

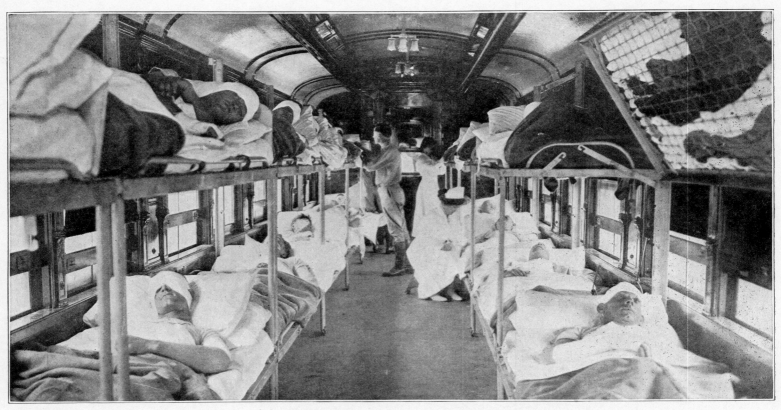

ALL IS NOT GLORY

Medical Officers' Training Camp at Fort Riley, Kansas. These soldiers are not wounded but afford practical experience in the handling of wounded men on board Hospital Trains. Red Cross nurses are in attendance.

PHYSICALLY FIT

Only a few months before, these boys were raw recruits with their civilian clothes and suitcases reporting for duty. Now they are finishing their training and will soon be on the look-out for the dreaded submarines.

GOOD-BYE, AMERICA

Forward-March! Training completed, the company takes a practice march preparatory to leaving for overseas. Large embarkation camps, housing 300,000 men, were constructed at New York, N. Y. and at Newport News, Va.

THE LAST ROUND-UP

Supply train at Camp Hancock, Ga., before leaving for Europe. The utmost secrecy surrounded all such movements.

THE YANKS ARE COMING

"We won't be back 'til it's over, over there."   The 42nd Division arriving at Brest.
Troopships being convoyed.

VIVE LA FRANCE

American infantry about to land on the soil of France. During the war, the United States Navy transported more than 2,000,000 men overseas, over 306,000 of them being carried to Europe during the one month of July, 1918.

FOOD FOR MEN AND GUNS

An indication of the huge amount of supplies it was necessary to send to France to keep the war machine going. Our cargo fleet reached 2,700,000 dead-weight tons and carried about 7,500,000 tons of material to Europe.

SO THIS IS ENGLAND

Americans passing through a typically English street in a large provincial town of the island empire. Even had the picture borne no label, the ivy-covered walls and the chimney pots would identify this as an English scene.

GREAT BRITAIN APPLAUDS

Men of the 4th Regiment, Air Service, pouring through the streets of an English seaport on their way to a troop-train bound for France. The U. S. air service was never large enough to protect our lines from enemy planes.

THE SHORES OF FRANCE

View of the harbor of Brest. Here many American doughboys first set foot on French soil. As they marched to camp, many could not help but wonder if this were their last, as well as their first, visit to this ancient city.

PRECIOUS CARGOES

Here, at the United States landing in Brest, the transports discharged their precious loads—men—food—clothing—guns—ammunition—medicine—supplies for engineers and signal corps—all the materials of war.

FIRST CAMP OF THE AMERICAN EXPEDITIONARY FORCE IN FRANCE
First U. S. Marines in France. Soon they were to attain fame in halting the last great German drive on Paris.

CHECK IN—CHECK OUT
Panorama of an American camp in France—the Second Depot. At a glance one can recognize, from the characteristically European architecture, that the scene presented here is not of a military camp anywhere in America.

FOUR STAR GENERALS
General Pershing with the Allied Commander, Marshal Foch
General Tasker H. Bliss   General Peyton C. March
American Representative on Allied War Council   Chief-of-Staff

FINISHING SCHOOL

Upon arriving in France, the outfits were sent to training schools. Machine Gun Company, 356th Infantry, 89th Division, at target practice just before a big drive. Near Boucq, Department of Meurthe et Moselle, France.

ADVANCE

After their training had been thoroughly completed, the new soldiers were sent on to the front lines. Here we see American infantrymen advancing in combat formation at the 1st Corps School, Gondrecourt, France.

IT WON'T BE LONG NOW

Training of the post-graduate type in France, (according to the text books). The picture shows an automatic rifle squad, with a scout, in correct position at an American military training camp near a provincial town in France.

PREPARING FOR TROUBLE

This photograph shows a class of army students being given a lesson in assembling the various parts of the Lewis machine gun. A graduate of this class could take a Lewis gun apart and reassemble it very speedily.

NOT LIKE BASEBALL

Because it was necessary to throw a grenade so that it would drop into the opposing trench, Americans, who were accustomed to throwing baseballs in a comparatively straight line, had to be taught a completely new technique.

UP AND AT THEM

Ring bayonet course—developing speed and perfect aim at the 1st Corps School in France. The ring was placed on the end of the arm which projects from the post and the object was to detach this ring without a miss.

THE TANK STOPPER

American infantrymen engaged in practice work at one of the big camps established by the United States Government in France. The gun shown in the picture is a "one pounder" which was effectually used against tanks.

GET THE FORM

Hand grenade practice, 2nd Battalion, 329th Infantry, 83rd Div. Soldiers were taught to lob the grenade up in the air so that it would land and stay on the blankets which were laid on the ground. Le Mans, Sarthe, France.

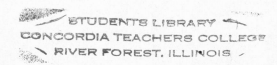

FIX BAYONETS

The boys in the Infantry were thoroughly instructed in the manipulation of the bayonet before they were sent on to the front line trenches. This photograph shows members of the 2nd Battalion, 329th Infantry, 83rd Division, practicing with their bayonets at Le Mans, Sarthe, France.

NEW FANGLED GADGETS

These men of the 144th Infantry, 36th Div., are engaged in rifle grenade practice at the 13th Training Section, Ville-sur-Tierre, France. The rifle grenade is made to accomplish the same purpose as the hand grenade but it is fired from the gun in place of being thrown by hand.

THE GUNNER AND THE LOADER

American military "finishing school" in France, situated in a section remote enough from the war area to make long continued practice of war maneuvers safe from interference by the enemy. Machine guns used in the war fired at the rate of between 450 and 500 rounds per minute.

LET THE WOMEN DO THE WORK

"Oh, it's tin, tin, tin, hunk o' tin. I've abused you and I've flayed you, but by Henry Ford who made you, you're a better man than I am, hunk o' tin." The picture shows French women in the service of the American army assembling "flivvers" overseas at an assembly plant.

FIRST VIEW OF THE ENEMY

A repair shop of the ordnance detachment of an American heavy artillery division. The men are looking at a German plane that is passing overhead and each one of them, obviously, would like to be able to take a shot at it.

THE MECHANICS DID THEIR BIT

This is not the village smithy but it is related to that ancient institution—it is the place near the Argonne where the tanks and the innumerable automobiles and motor trucks, required by modern warfare, were repaired.

TIME WAS IMPORTANT

Standard method of crating a heavy aviation truck for shipment to France or wherever Americans operated during the war. As the various parts of the machine were indicated on the crate, the trucks were easily assembled.

RATTA-TAT-TAT

The ancient craft of the cobbler was not to be despised in the work that was involved in keeping the American soldiers in the best of trim—he had to be fed, housed and clothed, and the latter item included good footwear.

ALL WORK AND NO PLAY MAKES JACK A DULL BOY

Baseball game between officers' teams, near Fere-en-Tardenois, arranged by Y. M. C. A. unit of 302nd Supply Train, 28th Div. Many organizations contributed in sending thousands of men and women and millions in dollars to France for the recreational needs of the soldiers.

KEEPING THEIR MINDS OFF THE WAR

When relieved of their regular duties, women, engaged in war work, enjoyed their leisure just as did the soldiers and sailors. Here is a group of women workers finding relaxation in an impromptu game of volley ball.

A LETTER FROM HOME

Letters from home for the soldiers in the field. Here we see the conditions under which the army mail clerks labored in distributing letters near the front. Mail for 27th Division, Corbie, Somme, France, Oct. 24, 1918.

THE MAID OF ORLEANS

This photograph was taken during scene four of the pageant "Jeanne d'Arc", which was presented for American soldiers by the Entertainment Section of the Y. M. C. A. in front of the Jeanne d'Arc church, near Domremy, France. The scene shows Jeanne in armor at Orleans.

CASEY AT THE BAT

"Uncle Joe" (J. F. Kerman, Utica, New York), a Knights of Columbus worker, giving aid to Maria Chausson, a French refugee, who was injured in La Basace. St. Pierremont, Department of Ardennes, France, November 7, 1918.

HOT DOUGHNUTS

These hardy American fighters, just in from the front line, are being given a fresh supply of doughnuts by members of that great institution which all veterans of the World War swear by—the Salvation Army. Varennes-en-Argonne, Department of the Meuse, France, October 12, 1918.

THE ARMY TRAVELS ON ITS STOMACH

Napoleon was right. Hungry soldiers in the line can stand the grind much better if they know that there will be food on hand when they are relieved. Supply Depot, 26th Division, Menil-la-Tour, France, May 25, 1918.

AWAITING THE SOLDIERS' RETURN

This spot was what the soldiers knew as a "ration dump." The seven immense army motor trucks are lined up to unload rations for the men on their return from the front lines where they have been fighting for several days.

THEY KNEAD THE DOUGH

The white bread of the American people was considered a delicacy by a great many of the soldiers of Europe. German raiding parties missed no opportunity of capturing whatever supplies of this food might be available.

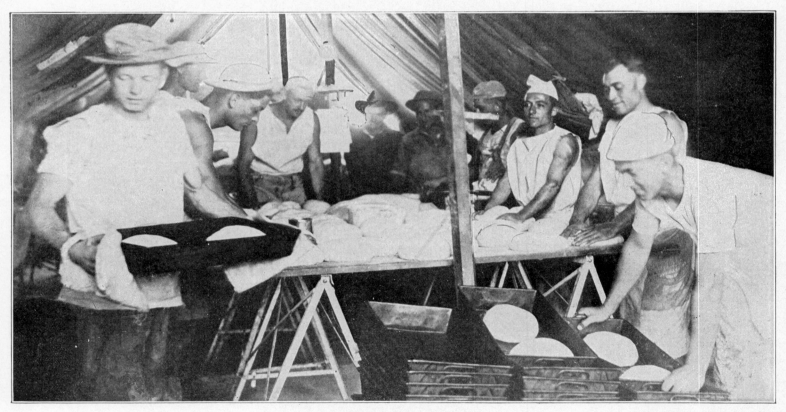

DOUGH THAT WAS DOUGH

American Bakery camp, near Dijon, Fr. Bread was an important medium of exchange in barter and trade operations.

BAKERIES, U. S. ARMY—BREAD! BREAD!

The labels on the big bags tell the story of the significance of this scene. How that legion of Americans did consume the staff of life! French girls are sacking 416 loaves of bread, 322nd Bakery Camp, near Dijon, France.

WHAT A PARTY

This was the largest mess kitchen to be established in France. It was located at Base Section No. 5, Brest, under the command of Capt. Shea, Q. M. C. On this occasion, October 29, 1918, 5,900 men were fed in 55 minutes.

THE KITCHENS MOVE UP—THIS MEANS ACTION

A concentration of rolling kitchens under the protection of the hill at Bouillonville, Department of Meurthe et Moselle, France. To the Yanks, Bouillonville was always known as "Souptown", the name which they gave the village when they arrived there for the first time.

COME AND GET IT

Kitchen No. 639, one of the rolling kitchens of S. S. U., with Cook Walter B. Brown seasoning the potatoes, Ippe-court, Department of the Meuse, France. These kitchens presented a constant target for the big guns of the enemy.

THE FOOD DETAIL

A dangerous bit of work. Company M, 102nd Infantry, near Aizy, France, carrying food along a communicating trench to the boys in the front line trenches. Food carriers were targets for the bullets of enemy snipers.

The Poilu Welcomes the Doughboy   Section of Trenches Through Cemetery Near Nancy

THE AMERICANS GO INTO THE TRENCHES

On the night of October 20, 1917, the men of the First Division having completed their training, relieved the French in the trenches southwest of Nancy. On the 27th of October, they captured the first German prisoner to be captured by American forces, and on November 3, the division suffered its first casualties from actual combat, three men of the 16th Infantry being killed by a German raiding party. This sector was no longer "quiet".

VETERANS NOW
On Jan. 18, 1918, the 1st Division moved into the front line trenches, Ansauville, relieving the 1st Moroccan Division.

THE GUN THAT FIRED THE FIRST SHOT FOR AMERICA
Battery C, 6th Field Artillery, 1st Division, fired America's first artillery shot against the German lines.

AND THEN CAME THE ENGINEERS

Pumping stations and reservoirs being erected by American engineers to supply drinking water for men and animals of a Yankee division, Euvezin, France. In some sections at the front, good drinking water was at a premium.

AQUA PURA—THE GREAT AMERICAN DRINK

Engineers building a reservoir. The picture recalls the declaration of a returned doughboy: "Engineers! You couldn't turn anywhere in France without seeing American engineers at work or seeing something they had done."

SOME DUGOUTS WERE MODERN

Electric light plant which supplied current for illuminating dugouts occupied by American troops near the River Meuse, France. The picture shows a motor and generator set up for an American division, near Vacherauville.

ROCKS FOR ROADS

Stone crusher operated by members of B Company, 28th Engineers, at Trondes, France. It is seen in use at one of the ballast quarries operated by the American army in France. Fight or work, the American boys were always there.

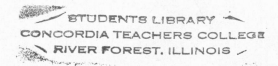

MUNITIONS MUST GET TO THE FRONT

View of a rock cut in France showing an American steam shovel at work. This is another detail of the extensive work done by American engineers to pave the way to Victory—a work accomplished with skill and efficiency.

LUMBERJACKS

French flat cars—rather a flimsy looking contrivance to the American accustomed to our solidly built railroad equipment—loaded with logs which are ready to be hauled to a French dock where they will be used for piling.

CLEAR ALL ROADS

This photograph shows some of the typical traffic troubles encountered in the advanced areas and illustrates the manner in which trucks are pulled out of shell holes by artillery tractors operated by American engineers.

BRIDGES MUST BE REBUILT

American lumbering camp in France. The picture shows members of a company of engineers loading piling on flat cars. At the right, background, are two piles of lumber which were "worked up" by Americans from native timber.

TAKE THE MESSAGE BACK

Here are two members of the Signal Corps with homing pigeons ready for maneuvers at a corps "school" in France. "They may get me," says the flyer over the German lines, as he releases a carrier pigeon from his plane. "You are a smaller bird and have a far better chance than I have of getting safely back to the base."

THE SIGNAL CORPS FOLLOWS

One of the tasks that fell to an American lineman, or signalman, on the Cambrai-St. Quentin front. This field telegraph expert, stringing wires on a "ready-made" telegraph pole near the front, is exposed to enemy fire.

TELEPHONE—TELEGRAPH—WIRES EVERYWHERE

American Signal Corps men of Headquarters, Second Army Corps, stringing telephone and telegraph cables through an ancient French village. They did their work expertly, being the pick of their profession in the U. S. A.

"THE NUMBER IS BUSY"

A group of American telephone girls who were designated a Signal Corps Telephone Unit. The work done by these brave and high-spirited girls was of the greatest importance in the complex military movements of our troops.

SUPPLIES MOVE TO THE FRONT

An endless chain of supplies of every description went forward to the American soldiers in the front lines in France. It was this generous and unceasing stream of American production that helped to maintain a high morale.

THERE IS GOING TO BE AN ATTACK

Tractors formed an important part of the army equipment in France. The picture shows tractors hauling American cannoneers and French 155 mm. guns along an apparently peaceful road. These tractors were made in France. Why!

HIDDEN FROM ENEMY AIR OBSERVERS

American artillery, well camouflaged, passing through Menil-la-Tour, France, en route to the Hindenburg Line. The picture reminds one of the line from Shakespeare's *Macbeth*—"Till Birnam Wood remove to Dunsinane."

LIFE BEGINS AT FORTY AND EIGHT

Forty Hommes—Eight Chevaux—Forty Men—Eight Horses—squeezed into French box cars. The men objected to such transportation but after they were packed in camions, they longed for the "comforts" of old Forty and Eight.

AT DUSK THE INFANTRY MOVES UP

American infantry walking up the railroad track on its way to the front in France. There was many a bleak stretch of devastated country surrounding these men who traveled thousands of miles to defend America's honor and ideals.

"FIFTY MILLION FRENCHMEN CAN'T BE WRONG"

Here we see a group of American soldiers, members of the 95th Company, Marines, 2nd Division, at Sommedieue, France, greeting their French brothers-in-arms as the latter march toward the fighting lines, April 29, 1918.

THE ARTILLERY GOES INTO ACTION AT DAWN

Battery F, 7th Field Artillery, 1st Div., in action. The photograph shows the camouflaged gun pits and dugouts, between Beaumont and Rambucourt, France. The trees in the background have been denuded of all their beauty.

THEY ENTER THE DRAMA
OF THE AGES

168th Infantry, coming over the top with sacks of hand grenades. Badonviller, March 17, 1918.

CONTACT WITH THE FRONT

117th Field Battalion Signal Corps. Companies B and C installing telephone lines to front line trenches by way of old culvert. Montigny, March 12, 1918.

A GOLD STAR FOR MOTHER

Burying an American soldier behind the lines, Menil-la-Tour, March 14, 1918.

Liquid fire machines brought back from No Man's Land by United States 18th Infantry after a raid on March 6, 1918. Menil-la-Tour.

Back view of liquid fire machines captured from Germans in raid of March 6, 1918. Menil-la-Tour.

ENEMIES AHEAD
Going on a raid of enemy trench to get a prisoner who will be "sweated" for information.

THE ZERO HOUR APPROACHES
168th Infantry, 3rd Battalion, American and French lieutenants cutting barbed wire preparatory to an infantry attack. Badonviller, March 17, 1918.

KNEE DEEP

Serg't Wm. Thorpe photographing in front line trenches. Photo Det. 26th Division. Beaumont, May 4.

A LEADER PASSES

General C. Edwards, Commanding 26th Division, paying last respects to Major R. Lufberry, 94th Aero Pursuit Squadron, near Toul, May 20, 1918. Major Lufberry, the American Ace, was killed Sunday, May 19, 1918.

BOUND FOR CANTIGNY

First trench mortar battery, 1st Division, Passing through a French village on the way to the front.

A FEW WERE SINGING

Co. A, 125th Inf., 32nd Div., passing border post when marching into Germany. Sentheim, May 29, 1918.

THE WORLD AWAITS THEIR FIRST TEST

Members of Battery E, 5th Field Artillery, 1st Division, on their way to front at Cantigny, May 27, 1918.

AMERICA SPEAKS

12th Artillery, Battery B, 2nd Division, camouflaged 75 mm. gun in action on American front.   Verdun, April 30.

POISON GAS

This startling photograph shows the effects of poison gas when gas masks were not worn. From 20 to 30 per cent of all our battle casualties were due to gas. There were so many false gas alarms and so many cases of "gas-jitters", that many justified alarms were not taken seriously.

CAVEMEN

Headquarters of the 6th Marines, 2nd Div., in smelly, bomb-proof dugouts, Sommedieue, France. There is a great contrast between the quiet activity of this picture and the feverish haste exhibited when the gas alarm sounded.

GAS ALARM

6th Marines, 2nd Div., responding to gas alarm, Verdun Sector, April 30, 1918. A few weeks before, under a severe artillery attack with gas shells, all officers and 230 men of one marine company had been gassed, 40 of the latter dying.

A RAIDING PARTY

Patrol of 168th Inf., under Lt. Curry, raiding enemy trench, near Badonviller, France, morning of March 18, 1918.

"WAS IST LOS?"

Snipers in camouflaged suits with camouflaged rifles. Inf. Bn. Headquarters, 42nd Div., Badonviller, May 18, 1918.

THE BIG GUNS ROAR
150th Field Artillery, 42nd (Rainbow) Division, firing barrage at 4:15 a.m. Reherrey, May 3, 1918.

PERHAPS HE HAD A MOTHER TOO

German killed by explosion shell at Cantigny where the 1st Division won the first All-American victory of the war.

SO THIS IS WAR

American field hospital in France. The photograph was taken as patients were being received from first aid stations farther toward the front. Months of hard training—a few minutes' fighting—then often death or this.

GOING UP EMPTY

Hospital Train No. 54, Horreville, France, April 26, 1918. The men are seen entering the cars, well supplied with stretchers which will come quickly into use as soon as the train has reached the neighborhood of field hospitals.

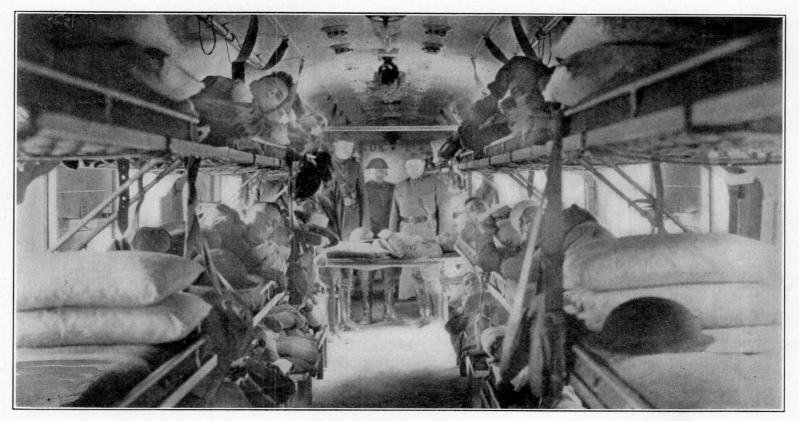

COMING BACK FULL

This is a view of the interior of the Hospital Train No. 54, after its arrival at its destination. The picture shows wounded men being brought aboard and placed in the bunks for their journey to a base hospital.

THEY WILL SOON BE GOING UP

Ambulance station and American ambulance company. At the right center, keen eyes may detect an ambulance, well-camouflaged. This camouflage was found necessary as at times, even the Red Cross didn't escape artillery fire. This station was located well back of the defense lines.

WE CAME BACK ALIVE

Here we see ambulances arriving with wounded American soldiers at an American field hospital in France. Many of our boys never came back.

THE HOSPITAL TRAINS ARE LOADED

Carrying wounded soldiers aboard a hospital train at Horreville, France. The wounded men, it is said, usually "registered" pleasure when they found themselves on the Hospital train, for that meant that they would soon be receiving care in a so-called comfortable bed at a base hospital.

WE WERE SHORT OF HOSPITAL TRAINS TOO

So wounded were loaded on flat cars and through rain, snow, wind, hail, cold or intense heat, began their long trek back. Some of them reached their destination alive. In this type of car, patients were placed in hammock beds.

AN OUNCE OF LUCK IS WORTH A TON OF PLUCK

View taken near Souilly, France, where Red Cross workers were distributing cakes and cookies to wounded Yanks on a hospital train. At Souilly were situated two great American evacuation hospitals, known as No. 6 and No. 7.

RED CROSS NURSES—WE SALUTE YOU

Wherever American soldiers went in Europe there, too, went American nurses. Literally thousands of wounded owe their lives to the courage, fortitude, devotion and skill of the nurses who cared for them. Unit T, American Red Cross Hospital, Mossley Hill, Liverpool, England.

HERE THE MAIMED WERE RECEIVED
Hospital at village Negre.   168th Infantry, 2nd Battalion.   Badonviller, April 29, 1918.

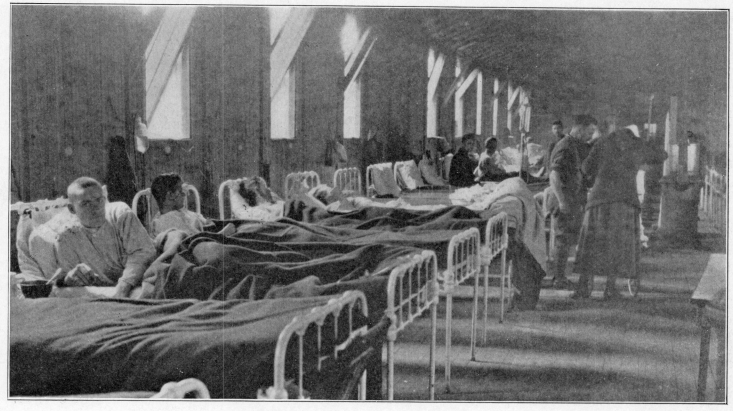

MANY A BOY LOST HIS MIND HERE
Base hospitals at their best are not good.   Thousands of cases of psychoneurosis developed in this environment.
The N. P.'s (neuropsychiatrics) in 1935 numbered 33,957.   The peak of these cases will not be reached until 1946.

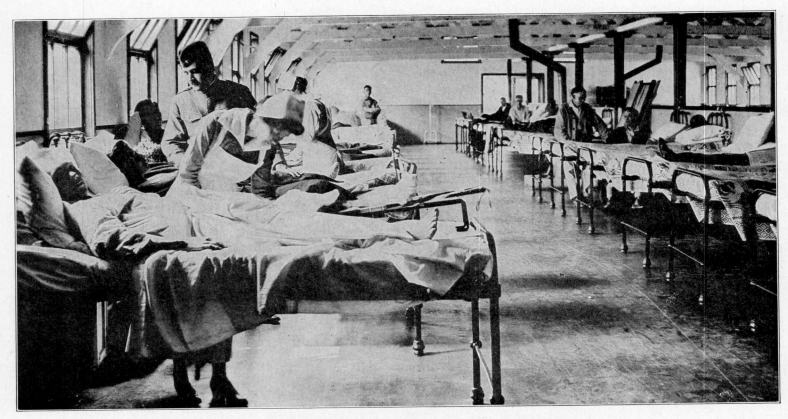

SHIPPED ACROSS THE CHANNEL FOR THE KNIFE

Ward G, Surgical Ward, American Red Cross Hospital, Mossley Hill, Liverpool, England. Wounded Americans were being attended by doctors and nurses. Here without the stimulus of conflict, nerves snapped and pain became unbearable.

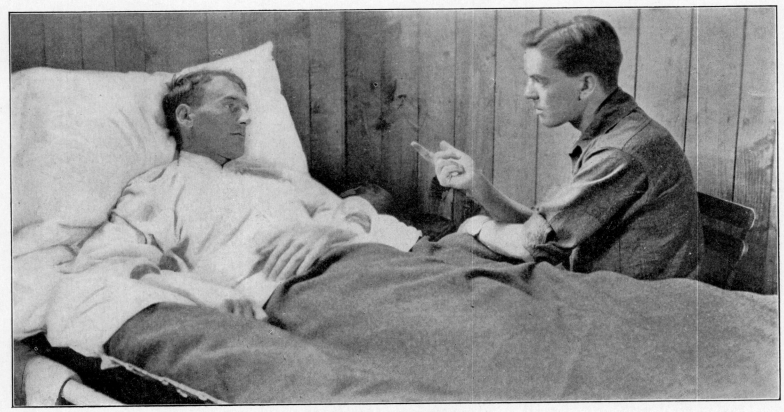

HIS NERVES ARE SHATTERED

One of the worst results of shell-shock is that it frequently leaves its victim with permanently shattered nerves. In numerous instances, hypnotism was found to be of value in aiding the sufferers to regain control of their nerves.

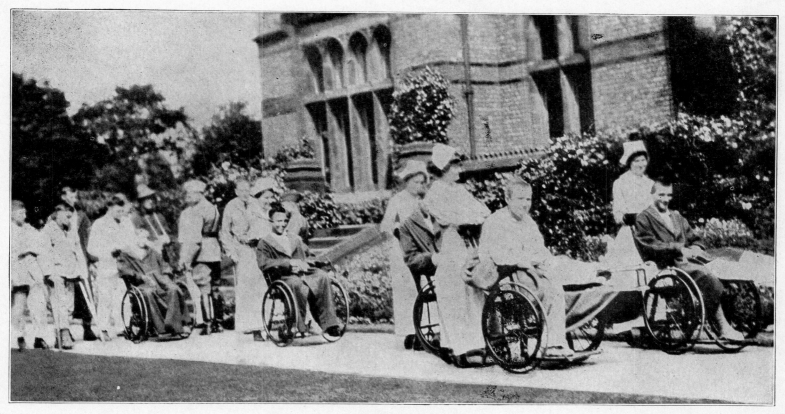

THEY SURVIVED

Wounded soldiers of American divisions being brought from France to "Blighty" which is the pet name of the British Tommie for home. This photograph was taken at the American Red Cross Military Hospital, Mossley Hill, Liverpool.

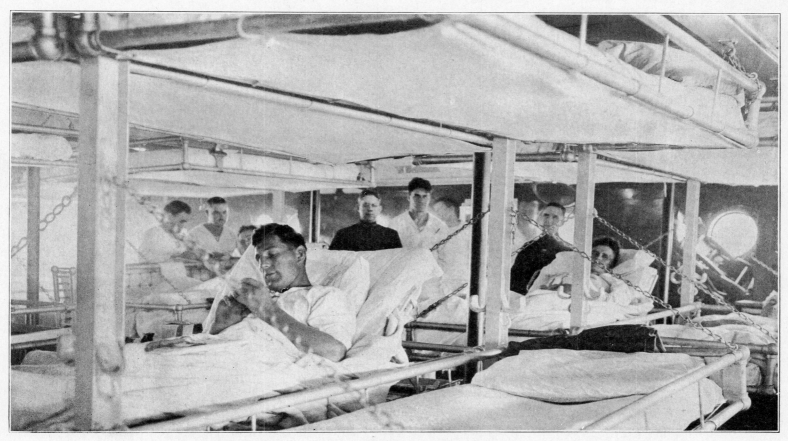

THE FIRST CARGO GOES HOME

As soon as it was possible to transport the wounded, they were shipped back to America to make room for the ever-increasing flow from the battlefield, back to the hospitals in Europe. Here are men on a hospital ship, going home.

THOSE WHO WERE NOT SHOT CAME BACK TO REST CAMP

Sometimes the rests camps were far enough back of the lines to make rest and relaxation possible. However, most of the "rest time" was spent in trying to find a piece of woods that was not occupied by another outfit. These men seem to have found a spot where they could recuperate,

HERE THE SOLDIER TRIED TO FORGET

Here is a hostess house where entertainments of varied character were arranged solely for the benefit of enlisted men; and not at infrequent intervals but at any time in the day. The problem was to find one when it was needed.

LIFE MUST GO ON

"Resting up" in an American infantry "sun parlor" in France. The roof is rather suggestive of the South Sea Islands, but it is a local attempt at a duplication of the thatched roofs common in some rural districts of France.

THEY ARE GETTING DELOUSED

American soldiers parading in clean underclothing to a tent where they will be given new outer garments. As the sign on the "hut" indicates, this is a Red Cross bathing and disinfecting plant. Camp de Gerard Sas, France.

DISCARDED BY THE DEAD AND THE DYING

Washers and extractors cleaning discarded clothing of American soldiers in France. This work, carried out under the direction of the Salvage Department, required an enormous equipment which was installed in record time.

IT'S SO PEACEFUL HERE

American soldiers at a beautiful river side in France. Many such charming spots were utterly destroyed in the war. The rest will be short. Soon the rolling kitchens will "roll out", which means, "we are going up again."

APPRECIATION OF WATER

Nothing was more appreciated by the soldier, when he was privileged to go back from the front line for a few days, than fresh water. Here the 80th Div. is cleaning up in the Ornain River. Water was scarce at the battle front.

IN THE DISTANCE—THE RUMBLE OF BIG GUNS

A beautiful scene on the River Meuse, in France—companion piece to hundreds that were forever wiped out of existence by the guns of the enemy and of the Allies who fought to drive him back. The men, resting in the boat and on the shore, are members of a company of American engineers,

ENJOYING A WELL-EARNED REST

The pleasant side of the Great War—from the standpoint of the American soldier. Two doughboys are seen fishing in the Lorraine River, one of the many beautiful streams of France. They are somewhat "shy" on regulation fishing lines and tackle but are having plenty of fun.

AND THESE DID NOT COME BACK

American cemetery located on the west side of Cuisy-Septsarges road. 4th Division, Cuisy, March 25, 1919.

ETERNAL REST IN THE TRENCHES WHERE THEY FELL

American graves in trench on southeastern edge of the Bois de Fays. Near Brieulles-sur-Meuse.

Members of the 11th Engineers, taken prisoners at Cambria Nov. 30, 1917 by the Germans.

THEY SAID THEY WERE GOING TO BERLIN, AND DID
They said they were going to Berlin, and were the first Americans to make it, but they went as prisoners.

THEY SAID THEY WERE GOING TO PARIS, AND DID
These Germans said they were going to Paris. They are—but as prisoners captured and escorted by Americans.

U. S. EXHIBIT A.

These wounded and disabled American soldiers were sent home to sell Liberty Bonds:

Front row:
    SERGEANT HALEY
    LIEUTENANT RODMAN
    PRIVATE SIMMS
Back row:
    PRIVATE JACOBSON
    SERGEANT JOLLY
    SERGEANT NOLEN

Parades Promoting Liberty Bond Sales Were Held All Over The Country

THE BOND SALESMEN

Frank Haley (lower left) was the first battle casualty invalided back to the United States. A member of the 11th Engineers, he was seriously wounded at Cambrai, November 30, 1917, when the Germans, in a surprise attack, came upon the men of the 11th, who were busy at their work, unarmed. They made a stout defense with spades, picks and such other construction tools as could be picked up. While eventually the majority of the men of the 11th succeeded in getting back to their base, the loss in killed, wounded and prisoners, was heavy.

As soon as these first casualties were able to leave the hospitals, the government sent them out to assist in the sale of Liberty bonds.

The theory was that when Mr. John Public, who had made no sacrifice, met these battle-scarred veterans, he would be shamed into supporting the government by buying Liberty Bonds. Incidentally the buying of these bonds was no sacrifice, as they proved to be the safest and most profitable investment. Purchasers got back their principal with interest, but the wounded soldiers, who assisted in their sale, got back neither their missing limbs nor their health.

INTELLIGENCE SECTION—FIRST DIVISION MAPPING THE MARNE SALIENT

On May 27, 1918, Ludendorff struck his third terrific blow between Soissons and Rheims. For 3 days, the average German advance was 10 miles a day. 40,000 prisoners and 400 guns were captured. Foch ordered the 2nd and 3rd American Divisions against the spearhead of the German rush.

"RETREAT! HELL NO WE JUST GOT HERE"

This was the reply given by Colonel (later Brigadier General) Manus McCloskey of the 12th Field Artillery, 2nd Division, when a French officer remonstrated with him: "Fini la guerre! (The war is finished). It is impossible to remain here; surely you are going to retreat."

FLEEING BEFORE THE INVADERS

The "quiet sector" of the Franco-British front from Reims to north of Soissons saw a terrific burst of fire at one A. M. on May 27, 1918. At 4:30 A. M., an overwhelming tide of grey swept over the trenches in the greatest surprise attack of the war. The American Intelligence Division had warned the French of the impending attack on May 14, only to be ridiculed. The sector was defended by four French and three British divisions, with only four divisions in reserve. As their remnants fled before the fifteen German divisions, with nine in reserve, five hundred thousand residents of the territory fled from their homes in panic.

SHELLS SCREAMING OVERHEAD

The Americans advanced down roads choked with the debris of the French-English army and the civilians, forced to leave their old homes between sunrise and sunset A stream of weary humanity — old men — little children — women carrying babies — trudged on with horror in their eyes, clutching a few odd household effects which they had picked up.

GOING NOWHERE

These poor unfortunates had no destination—no plans. Behind them the great German army, advancing ten miles per day, surged as a tidal wave, over 650 square miles of territory, engulfing everything in its path. In front of them every bit of shelter was occupied. Two million homeless refugees were in the exodus of 1914—Now another half million—No homes to go to—No schools for the children—No doctors for the sick— —No extra supplies of food to meet the unusual demand—Sorry was the plight of the refugees.

CLEAR THE ROADS

A tidal wave of Germany's best—24 divisions, with the greatest artillery preparation ever effected, has been thrown against the 11 Allied divisions in this sector. The 3rd Division was ordered to the bridgeheads at Chateau-Thierry; the 2nd Division to the edge of Belleau Woods.

NO SMOKING—NO TALKING

Members of the 30th Infantry, 3rd Division, passing through the streets of Viels-Maisons, June 2, 1918, en route to Chateau-Thierry. They had been shelled on the previous night and no one had run away. They were ready.

A HARD GAME—WAR

A few, exhausted, fell by the roadside. An all-night ride in a camion. An all-day forced march through showers of rain with hot sunshine between—uniforms steamed and thirst was torture. A swift pace and little rest.

LIKE INDIANS ON THE MARCH

A machine gun battalion of the 3rd Division passing through a small French village on their way to Chateau-Thierry with orders: "Hold at all costs." Here the Americans piled the German dead in heaps around the bridgeheads, but to the Northwest the enemy was still coming.

THE GUNS MUST BE FED

These are 155 mm. shells to be used by the big guns when they arrive at the Chateau-Thierry neighborhood. However, the Germans were pouring through and the American Division went into action before the heavy artillery arrived.

A MEAN RECEPTION

Here is a 5-inch gun battery, cleverly concealed, which was captured after doing its share of damage. Iron-souled Prussian gunners—they had such men—met the bayonet and died that way. A gunner can be seen dimly in the rear.

ROADS MUST BE REPAIRED

Company C, 23rd U. S. Engineers, busy unloading stone for the repair of shell-torn roads, which must be put in good condition and made ready for the counter-offensive which is being planned by the Allied high command.

THE BEGINNING OF THE EBB TIDE

From June 27, when Ludendorff began his great drive on Paris, until July 21, when the Germans were forced to evacuate Chateau-Thierry, the town was a slaughter house. American participation and sacrifice had turned the tide.

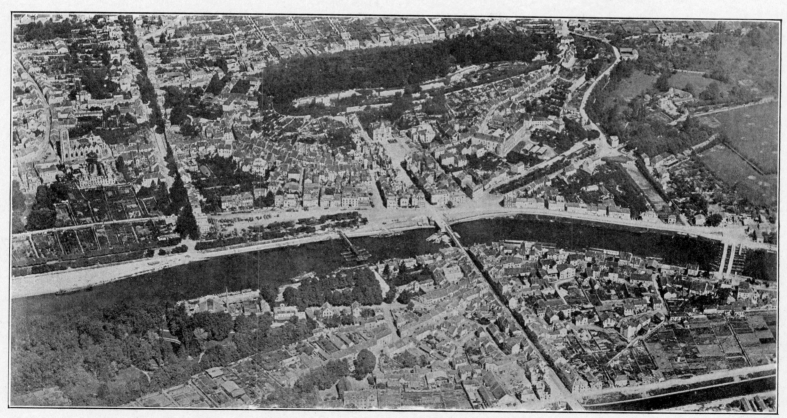

A GHOST CITY

During the German occupation of Chateau-Thierry, this city was looted. Fine furniture, pictures and libraries, dating back to the empire period, were forever ruined. What was not carried away, was destroyed beyond all use.

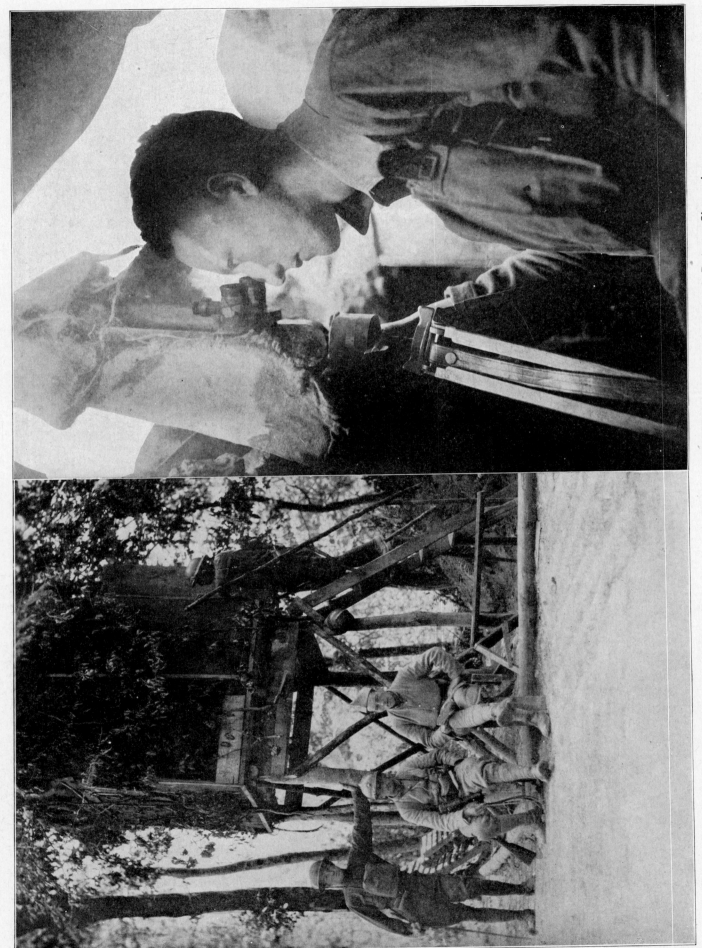

Camouflaged Observation Post   Trench Periscope Observation

THE 32nd DIVISION GOES INTO THE LINE

While the 2nd and 3rd Divs. were stopping the last great German drive on Paris, the 32nd Div. (Michigan and Wisconsin N. G.), held the first lines in the Haute-Alsace Sector against combined assaults by larger forces, May 18 to July 21. Then they were transferred to Chateau-Thierry.

Member of Company B, 127th Infantry, on duty in observation post, near Altkirch, Carspach Woods, June 6, 1918.

Member of 127th Infantry, 2nd Battalion, 32nd Division, on duty at Lock 25 on canal at Eglingen, June 6, 1918.

This point is defended by men who were aboard the English Transport Tuscania when it was torpedoed off the British Coast, Feb. 5, 1918. Thirteen men of the 32nd Division were drowned as the transport sank.

CAME THE DAWN TO BELLEAU WOOD

June 6, 1918. As the dawn came, the 3rd Div. moved out of these woods in 4 waves—a French formation, based on the theory that the 4th wave might reach the objective—the Marines never used it again. Men turned to look as a German shell burst in a field—many looked no more.

FIFTY BATTERIES WERE WORKING ON THE WOODS OF BELLEAU

Capt. Hyatt, with megaphone, of Battery F, 15th F. A., (Light), 2nd Div., receiving reports from observation posts on the effectiveness of his fire. The platoons, very lean now, advanced through the woods filled with shrapnel.

BATTLE-SIGHT—FIRE AT WILL

Day and night for nearly a month, they fought in corpse choked underbrush with rifle, bayonet, machine gun and bomb. Belleau Woods, torn by shell, covered with debris of war, was won by inches, the capture being completed on June 26.

CURTAIN OF NIGHT

Shells burst as the files went down the road. As twilight fell, what remained of the divisions came out of their shell holes. Belleau Wood had been won at a terrific price, adding another glorious chapter to American history.

MANY WERE ABSENT AT ROLL CALL

The next morning, out of range of enemy shell fire, Major C. T. Holcomb, commanding 2nd Battalion, 6th Marines, 2nd Division, called a halt for a moment's rest. This photograph shows all that remained of the battalion.

"FIRST-AID, FOR THE LOVE OF GOD"

First-aid station, Battery A, 6th F. A., Bonvillers, June 10, concealed from enemy observation by trees and camouflage, receiving wounded who were able to get back. After first-aid was given, they were sent to field hospitals.

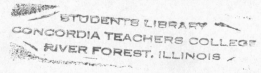

THE GUESTS ARRIVE

Marines, 4th Brigade, arriving at 15th Field Hospital, near Montreuil-aux-Lions. Wounded men did not seem to suffer much at first. The impulse of the attack and the shock from the missile, numbs the nerves. Later, the pain becomes unbearable. Men break before reaching the hospitals.

"FIRST-AID, THIS WAY"

In the darkness of night, litter-bearers in response to the pitiful wail, "First-aid, this way!", crawled through the fields which were drenched with blood. Hundreds of men were lying where guns had cut them down.

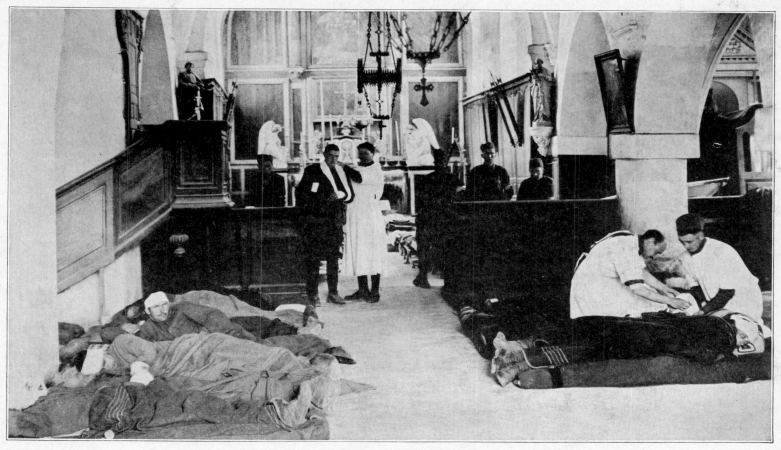

IN GOD'S TABERNACLE

1st Field Hospital Unit of the 2nd Division at Bezu, France, June 16, 1918, in the interior of medieval church. Here men suffered and died, or lived in the constant and nerve-racking fear of bombs from enemy planes.

MEN WALKED SILENTLY, REMEMBERING THE DEAD LEFT IN THE WOODS

What remained of the 1st Battalion, 4th Brigade, 5th U. S. Marines, 2nd Div., after two replacements. After 38 days' attacking from Hill No. 142 on the left, through what the French now call Bois de la Brigade de Marine, to Vaux on the right, these men are now going back to rest camp.

VETERANS NOW

After 38 days of living hell, the American Marines, 2nd Division, under the cover of darkness, silently wend their way back to a rest camp, knowing that it will not be long before they will be called to go up to the front again.

RUMORS AFLOAT

"Hey, Buddy! Did you hear that we were going to be sent to Paris to parade in the Frenchmen's Fourth of July— Bastille Day, they call it." Such rumors, alive in rest camps, kept the mind off the dirty business still ahead.

LUCKY TO BE CAPTURED BY AMERICANS

It is generally recognized that the personal hatred which the Allied soldiers had for the German was not shared by the American soldier, despite the fact that the instructors sent to the U. S. training camps by the foreign governments constantly worked to instill such hatred.

COMRADES

"Fifty-fifty" was the motto adopted by doughboys in France—that is, in their relations with the civil population. The Yank and the French boy are pals, sharing food and playing together and each, a teacher of languages.

ASSISTING THEIR ALLIES

American boys in rest camps were always willing and anxious to "lend a helping hand" to the French peasant woman, whose men folks were either at the front, fighting, or had gone on that long journey from whence no traveler ever returns. No task was too lowly for the Yankee soldier.

NEW DIVISIONS GOING UP

While those who had fought in Belleau Wood and Chateau-Thierry were resting, newly arrived divisions were going to the front. Here, the "Veterans" are giving the merry ha-ha to recruits who must learn what it is all about.

Soldier of 125th Infantry with a supply of grenades, Near Guewenheim, Alsace, June 24, 1918.

Members of Company A, 126th Infantry, 32nd Division, on duty at outpost. Left to right: Jos. Brust, private, and Garford Wood, private. Hecken Sector, Alsace, June 14, 1918.

Machine gun emplacement arranged to protect an observation post. 126th Infantry. Dieffmatten, June 26, 1918.

Advanced observation post held by Company I, 126th Infantry. This post is one of the most advanced in this sector, and was formerly a German machine gun emplacement. 32nd Division, Dieffmatten, June 27, 1918.

Anti-aircraft machine gun placed to protect gun positions. Battery A, 120th F. A. Bourbach-le-Bas, June 25.

Soldier of the 125th Infantry, using periscope to obtain view of No Man's Land. Near Guewenheim, June 25, 1918.

A few of the parts of an airplane which remained above ground. Photograph lens found in the wreckage unbroken. Plane brought down by French anti-aircraft guns. 77th Division, La Chapelle, July 5, 1918.

ON THE ALERT

Member of Company B, 325th Infantry, 82nd Division, in our last outpost No Man's Land, Regnieville, July 1.

ENEMY TANKS APPROACH

French "37", a one-pounder, in firing position on parapet in second line trench. This gun has a maximum range of a mile and a half, is more accurate than a rifle, and is capable of firing 28 rounds a minute. Headquarters Company, 126th Infantry. Dieffmatten, June 25, 1918.

LET THEM HAVE IT

Early in the war, only high explosive shells were used in trench mortars. Because of their large shell capacity, they were later adopted for launching gas attacks, frequently being lined up hub to hub.

Mud and water in the trenches made the operation of these mortars extremely difficult.

"THE FROGS' FOURTH OF JULY"

July 14, Bastille Day, found the Marines swimming in the Marne. Cannons seemed louder this day toward Rheims. That night, 9-inch shells began dropping in Croutte-sur-Marne. The eastern sky was aflame with gun flashes.

WE MUST BE GOING SOMEWHERE

Beans for breakfast. At dusk, bugles blew, "Assembly." The companies started down the river road and met other outfits. "Where are you tramps going?" "Don't know, and don't care, but you notice we're leading as usual."

"THEY RODE US TO CHATEAU-THIERRY IN THEM BUSSES"

"And it was a one-way trip for a lot of us." The Great German Friedensturm (peace offensive), was on. Midnight, Sunday, July 14, German artillery opened the battle to determine the fate of Paris, and the Marines are going up.

AMERICANS IN THE PATH

1st Co., 102nd M. G. B., 26th Div., going into action, July 19. Repulsing the German attempts to cross the Marne, the 3rd Div. stood the brunt of the attack. The 28th Div. was forced to withdraw to heights south of the Marne.

STOPPING THE DRIVE

Artillery, 1st Div., changing positions at Soissons. After 3 days of terrific fighting, it was apparent that the great "peace offensive" was collapsing. The Germans advanced only 6 miles, being driven back by the 28th Div.

AS THE EARTH TURNS

103rd Infantry, 26th Div., jumping off, 4:30 A.M., July 18. They did not stop until they had captured Torcy, Belleau and Givry. On the 24th, they occupied a line in the Foret de Fere, where they were relieved by the 42nd Div.

INTO THE VALLEY OF ADVENTURE

Skirmish line of the 103rd Infantry, 26th Div., advancing toward Torcy, 4 A.M., July 18. American troops, numbering 85,000, were fighting the Second Battle of the Marne, and the offensive was now passing into Allied hands.

KAMERAD!

Over 1,500 Germans realized their ambition to reach Paris during the Friedensturm, but they went as prisoners of war. A year after our entry into the war, 250,000 American troops were in France. Now, 10,000 are arriving daily.

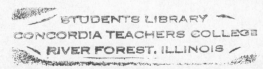
159

"MY MOTHER WILL NEVER FIND MY GRAVE HERE"

Through dense thickets, foul with odors—this ground changed hands many times—the Americans advanced. By Aug. 1, over a million of them were in France. America was about ready to have an independent army of her own.

ENEMIES AHEAD

Germans in trenches at Soissons. The Americans can be seen advancing up the slope. The American Intelligence Division secured more than 17,000 photographs of enemy positions. How they were secured is another story.

THEY'RE ON THE RUN

The Germans met something new—American rifle fire that killed at 800 yds. On the June drive toward Paris, the Germans captured 55,000 prisoners, 650 guns, and occupied 650 sq. m. of territory, from which they are being driven.

THESE DID NOT RUN

Fearless Prussians—there were many such—met bayonet with bayonet and died that way defending this trench mortar position at the edge of a wood north of Cierges, Aug. 13. The 125th Inf., 32nd Div., captured the position.

THE RAINBOW

Company H, 167th Inf., 42nd (Rainbow) Div., in dugouts near Rheims. On the defensive, they prevented capture of Rheims, took the offensive on the 26th. Two men were killed by enemy shells five minutes after photo was taken.

"ONE HELUVA BUSINESS"

On the 26th, the 42nd Div. seized Croix Rouge Farm, and crossed Ourcq River. July 29th, aided by 4th Div. units, they captured Sergy, Meurcy Farm, Seringes-et-Nesles, advancing on the 30th to Foret de Nesles and beyond Sergy.

COMBAT FORMATION

The 29th Div., Brigadier-General Charles W. Barber commanding, going into action in Haute-Alsace sector. While the fierce battle raged around Soissons, action was heavy on all fronts. New divisions were getting the baptism of fire.

THE GORY ROAD

Sunken road used by Germans as a trench and trench-mortar position against 16th Inf., 1st Div., Pleissy, France, July 18, 1918. Aided by 1st French Moroccans, Brezy-le-Sec was captured; Soissons was reached night of the 22nd.

WAS IT A HOLIDAY?

Companies M and K, 326th Inf., 82nd Div., advancing on enemy positions through clouds of poison gas, Choloy, France, Aug. 1, 1918. This division of men from Georgia, Alabama, Florida and Tennessee, had 7,336 casualties.

FOREVER AFTER

Gas patients of 82nd and 89th Divs., Aug. 1, 1918, exposed to the elements because facilities in 326th Field Hospital were inadequate for huge number of patients. Many of the after effects of gas are still unknown to medical science.

SCIENCE AT BAY

Gas Ward, Field Hospital No. 326, near Royaumeix. German chemical warfare, introduced to French, April, 1915, created problems which still baffle medical science. Tuberculosis and other terrible diseases follow in the wake of gas.

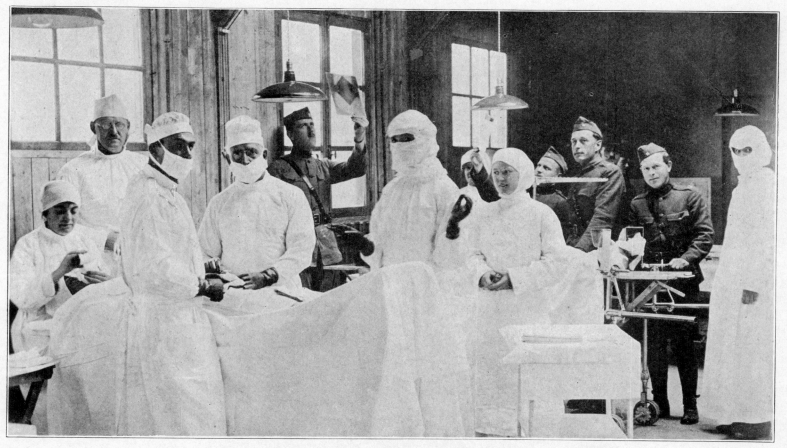

"DEATH FOLLOWS A FORMULA"

Suffering boys' nerves were "shot" in the operating room of a hospital unit. Anaesthetics were frequently unavailable; gangrene and osteomyelitis sometimes developed. Here many of our boys went shrieking into the Great Beyond.

THE DANCE OF FIRE

A patrol of 166th Inf., 42nd Div., in Villers-sur-Fere, July 30, 1917, sniping at enemy machine gun nests. Machine gun units, manned by strong-hearted Germans, were left to protect the retreat to the Hindenburg line and check the American advance. Most of these gunners died at their posts.

COMING OUT

The 26th Infantry, 1st Division, coming out of the lines near Fresnes, July 31, 1918, pass through the shell swept streets. They are spaced so that one shrapnel burst can not include more than one group.

THESE DID NOT COME OUT

French mothers pay their respects to the sons of American mothers.

THE WAR MOVES ON

Co. A, 6th Engineers, 3rd Division, constructing a combination trestle bridge across the Marne River, east of Chateau-Thierry. This bridge was constructed for the use of Franco-Americans in the offensive that drove the enemy back to the Vesle River. Mezy, France, July 24, 1918.

EVERYWHERE—ENGINEERS

Steam shovel and dump cars of 16th Engineers, on embankment between the canal and the Loire River, Nevers cut-off, Nevers, France. Although often prosaic, the work of the engineers was of utmost importance in winning the war.

BARBED WIRE FOR DEFENSE

Advance engineer's dump. Maj. Pugh, 21st Engineers, and Capt. Crofton, Headquarters, Department of Light Railways and Roads, near Nauginsard. An American offensive is in preparation. Barbed wire and other supplies are sent up.

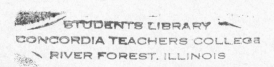

MOMENTS THAT TRY MEN'S SOULS

28th Division, throwing hand grenades, advancing against the town of Fismette, which was captured August 22, 1918. Heavy casualties were suffered by these National Guard troops from Pennsylvania as a result of a counter-attack.

Tragedy of Fismette
Due to Interference of French General

The following report is from the war memoirs of Major General R. L. Bullard, U.S.A.:—

"In Fismette, the portion of the village of Fismes on the north side of the Vesle, I had a single company of infantry, 150 men of the 28th (Pennsylvania) Division. One day I was ordered to make a raid with this company. It was made with great determination, but the bluffs of the river to the east, north and north-west were lined with enemy machine guns, and the company, thus covered on three sides by the enemy's fire, had no success. It was driven back into its cellars in Fismette.

"This company could be reinforced and fed at night only across a broken bridge, now not even a foot-bridge. This crossing was swept from two directions by enemy machine-gun fire, and men crossed, whether by day or night, only at intervals, and then only a man at a time. In short, men could not cross. It was evident that whenever the enemy desired he could wipe out the company on the north bank of the Vesle.

"After its failure in the raid, as ordered by our French general, I ordered that company withdrawn to the south bank of the Vesle River, man by man, at night. My chief-of-staff, who was very much in favor of the general's idea of bridge-heads, knew of the order which I was going to give. When I returned from Fismes late in the afternoon, I found our French general at my corps headquarters, and that my chief-of-staff had informed him of my order

to withdraw the company. The French army commander ordered me at once to replace it. It was done.

"Three or four days after this affair, without my ability to reinforce it or save it, completely at the mercy of the enemy, this company was wiped out by an enemy attack. Then I noticed that the French communique of the day reported that my 3rd Corps had repulsed an enemy attack. When the French army commander appeared at my corps headquarters he offered me as consolation for his error this French communique. It was at least acknowledgment of the responsibility for the mistake.

"But it did not console me for the only accident of my military career. I reported it at once to the American Commander-in-chief, General Pershing.

"A few days later I saw General Pershing himself. He told me that he had seen the letter, that he understood. He was much irritated, and asked me with vehemence: 'Why did you not disobey the order?'

"I did not answer. It was not necessary to answer. The general had spoken in the vehemence of his irritation."

Author's note: The raid referred to was not a raid but an attack. This little band of men was sent against the German army. As in the "Charge of the Light Brigade"—some one had blundered.

Night attack with phosphorous bombs against the 28th Division, Fismette, August 26, 1918.

The 28th Division meeting gas attack on the banks of the Vesle, August 23, 1918.

REINFORCEMENTS STOPPED

Main bridge between Fismes and Fismette, referred to by General Bullard in his report of the Tragedy of Fismette.

ONE MINUTE BEFORE THE BARRAGE OPENED

As dawn broke on the morning of Aug. 22, Battery C, 56th Artillery, Sergeant C. Swan and crew of Gun No. 1, opened the barrage. The Germans were now committed to the defensive, the offensive having passed to the Allies.

THE DOODLE-BUG

This photograph shows a tank advancing, as quickly as possible, through a French village to assist the doughboys in crossing the Vesle River. By September 1, 1918, one and a quarter million American soldiers were in France.

SHOT FROM THE REAR

Being shot from the rear while advancing—not retreating—was a rather unusual experience in war. After the Americans had proceeded up the St. Quentin Canal, the Germans emerged from a tunnel and attacked them from the rear.

THE SON OF AN AMERICAN PRESIDENT

Grave of Lieutenant Quentin Roosevelt, who died "in aerial combat, July 14, 1918, for Right and Liberty." The Sixth French Army, aeronautical section, paid a graceful tribute to the memory of the American aviator by erecting this cross headboard and fence on his grave, near Chamery.

MAKING LITTLE ONES OUT OF BIG ONES

Showing small stones being wheeled onto the road to fill up chuck holes caused by heavy traffic of war. Men at right background, are breaking the stones into small pieces. Capt. Miller and Lt. Bliss, 308th Engs. are shown.

WE MODERNS?

This Dinky Engine of the 308th Engineers, 83rd Division, hauls the stone for building roads from a quarry three kilometers from the unloading point. Capt. Edward K. Miller is in charge, Sergy, France, August 27, 1918.

THE DOGS OF WAR

Members of the 77th Division, with their messenger dogs, in the Oise-Aisne operations where they relieved the 4th Division on the Vesle River, August 11, 1918. They crossed, on September 3, in the face of heavy machine gun and battery fire. The Division's casualties totaled 9898.

AIRPLANE SPOTTER

Working with balloon observers and the ground crew, this look-out scans the horizon for enemy planes. The moment that one is detected the balloon is hauled to safety as observation balloons are helpless before enemy aircraft.

GAS FOR BLIMPS

American engineers erecting a huge tank and hydrogen plant for the manufacture and storage of gas to be used in military balloons, at an aviation experiment station. The United States Army had 77 balloons, with 252 observers, actually at the front during period of hostilities.

GROUND CREW

Moving kite balloon into open, preparatory to sending it aloft. Artillery fire in World War was mostly "blind," directed at targets out of the gunners' sight. Observers in captive balloons directed the fire by telephone.

EYES OF THE ARTILLERY

American observation balloon directing fire of French artillery, seen scattered about the fields in background. In foreground, 308th Engs., 83rd Div., are repairing the road between Bethincourt and Cuisy, Meuse, Oct. 5, 1918.

HAPPY LANDING

Captive balloon of 3rd Balloon Company, 3rd Corps, being brought safely to earth after period of observation near Mallancourt, Meuse, Oct. 1, 1918. Ground crews could bring down balloon quickly when enemy planes were sighted.

REEL TRUCK AND CREW

The reel truck controls the flight of a kite balloon. It serves as an anchor when the balloon is stationed in the air, changes its location whenever it is necessary, and hauls it down when the period of observation is over.

READY TO SOAR

An observation balloon being taken from its camouflaged home in a wood in France. These balloons were carefully guarded, as a shot was likely to explode the gas and set them on fire, causing a loss of thousands of dollars.

A FLAMING METEOR

Balloon of the 6th Balloon Company down in flames on the road between Cuisy and Montfaucon, Meuse, Oct. 3, 1918. The American observers took to their parachutes and landed safely. Balloon service lost 45 balloons in the war.

GOING UP

Crew of an observation balloon in the basket ready to ascend. One member wears a telephone headset for use in reporting the observations. Note the ballast that is being attached to the basket for use in regulating the height of the ascent, Brouville, France, April 23, 1918.

SAFE FROM PRYING EYES
Camouflaged covering for walks and huts at 25th Division Headquarters. Boucq, April 30, 1918.

THE DEAR DARK WOODS
Fourth Army Headquarters, showing the camouflage over the building. 4th Army Corps, Boucq, Oct. 14, 1918.

CAMERA OBSCURA

Lenses, placed under the aperture in the roof of the building, reflect the course of the plane flying overhead. The course is recorded on a mapping board. By the use of this device it was possible to tell where an enemy plane was heading, and send fighting planes to drive it back.

FLIGHT SECTION—A. E. F.

Panoramic views of planes in readiness to take off. Some planes were equipped with cameras, by which the enemy positions were photographed. There were 740 American planes in action, with 757 pilots and 481 observers.

SPEED

As soon as air views were taken, they were rushed to headquarters so that commanding officers could know the lay of the land inside the enemy's lines. Here a motorcycle courier is waiting to receive the very important films.

THE CAMERA EYE

Member of Royal Flying Corps, B. E. F., demonstrating camera used for taking aerial reconnaissance photographs. Loaded cameras were operated by pressing a button, when over enemy territory. American aviators made 6,672 observation flights and took 17,845 pictures of German positions.

CLIPPED WINGS

Wreck of an airplane used by American aviators in France, after a 500 foot drop. In this instance the lucky pilot escaped uninjured, but official reports show that 586 American aviators were killed, wounded and missing.

CRACK-UP

All that remained of a Sopwith plane used by Americans. This machine crashed near Tours, France, Oct. 10, 1918. The pilot was killed and the observer seriously injured. The American Air Service in France lost 271 planes.

FALLEN EAGLE

German observation plane forced down in Toul by Capt. C. J. Biddle, 13th Aero Squadron, Aug. 17, 1918. Observer was shot through stomach and killed; pilot was uninjured. According to official figures, American aviators destroyed 845 enemy planes, 491 confirmed, 354 unconfirmed.

NO SMOKING ALLOWED

Filling aerial bombs with the stuff that scatters men and munitions all over a forty-acre lot. American aviators conducted about 150 raids, in which they dropped over 275,000 pounds of high explosives on the enemy objectives.

CONTACT

Eleven single-seater flying planes ready to start on an offensive patrol from Oudezeele at 4:15 P. M., Aug. 18, 1918, under command of 1st Lt. Reed. American pilots spent 35,849 hours in the air over the enemy lines.

THE NAVY LEARNS TO FLY

Students of Naval Aviation School at Pensacola, Fla., pulling plane up runway after a practice flight. Naval Aviation Force during the war reached about 40,000 men equipped with 1,170 flying boats, 695 seaplanes, 262 land planes, 10 free balloons, 205 kite balloons, 15 dirigibles.

BOLTS FROM THE BLUE

Most Americans in France were entirely too familiar with the results of aerial bombs but few knew what they looked like before they exploded. Here are four different types pictured with a bluejacket to show the different sizes.

MORE PLANES FOR THE NAVY

Naval aviation mechanics assembling flying boats at a base port in France. The airplane was indispensable for spotting U-boats lying beneath the surface. Navy planes attacked 43 submarines, sinking 4 and damaging others.

A CRUISER OF THE SKIES

Although slower than the airplane and more vulnerable, the naval dirigible was an important weapon against the submarine because of its ability to stay aloft for long periods. Dirigibles were used for convoy and patrol duty.

"STAND BY"

Trying to get a line on a German submarine. The look-out on this destroyer has called a warning and the gun crew have hopped to their stations, anxious to catch sight of the telltale periscope amid the rolling waves.

THE SEAS GIVE UP THEIR DEAD

Sailors from the U. S. Fleet stationed at Queenstown, Ireland, visiting a spot that will always remain sacred in American history—the burial place of the victims of the Lusitania disaster, located on the outskirts of Queenstown.

THE NAVY'S HOME IN EUROPE

Here is a view of Queenstown, Ireland, the place where the first United States warships in European waters reported on May 4, 1917. Later on in the war this city became the largest American naval base on foreign soil.

THE RETURN OF THE MAYFLOWER

A painting by Bernard F. Gribble, showing arrival of the first American destroyers off the coast of Ireland. They were the Wadsworth, Porter, Conyngham, McDougal, Davis and Wainwright, under command of Lieut. Com. J. K. Taussig. The painting is now the property of Admiral Sims.

SHORE LEAVE

A few of the 600,000 Americans engaged in naval activities during the war. This boatload of "gobs" is from the United States Cruiser Melville, flag-ship of the fleet of destroyers stationed at Queenstown, Ireland. Many of these boys are of Irish descent and are now off to see their ancestral homes.

MUSTERING THE SHORE PATROL

This Seaman's Guard is ready to start patrolling the streets of Queenstown. It was their unpleasant duty to see that only those with leave were ashore and that none of the boys overstayed when their leave had expired.

GOLD FISH AND HARDTACK

The United States Naval Storehouse at Queenstown, Ireland. When one considers in how many places it was necessary to expend vast sums for the maintenance of war equipment, the purpose of the Liberty Loans is evident.

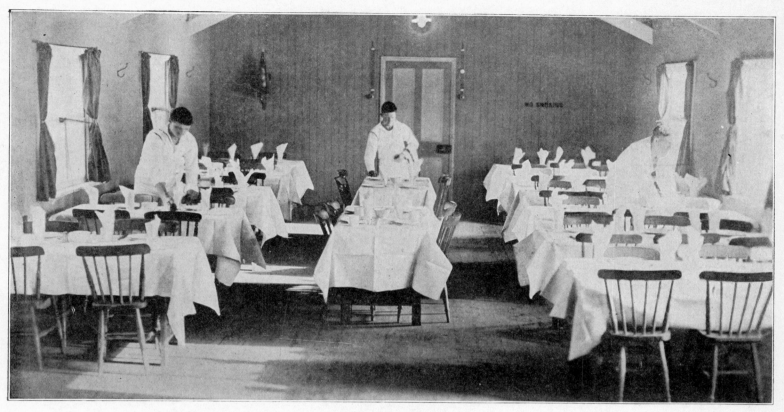

LUXURY FOR SAILORS

While not so ornate as most clubs, this dining room of the Naval Men's Club at Queenstown was much more comfortable than the regular mess rooms on destroyers, submarines, and submarine chasers where the men ate when at sea.

"THE FLEET'S IN"

Bluejackets relaxing in the pleasant reading room of the U. S. Naval Men's Club in Queenstown. Recreation facilities of this kind helped to build up the morale and maintain the high efficiency of the American naval forces.

NAVAL HOSPITAL AT QUEENSTOWN

Sailors, as well as soldiers, were subject to wounds, injuries, and illness. The Bureau of Medicine and Surgery, under Rear Admiral William C. Braisted, established four naval hospitals at the base ports in the British Isles.

WINNING THE BATTLE AGAINST DEATH

Interior of a U. S. Naval Hospital. During the war the capacity of naval hospitals was increased from 3,850 beds to 15,689. Navy Medical Dept. also took care of the Marines in France and all soldiers while on the high sea.

JOURNEY'S END

Pulling into the harbor at Brest meant the end of the trip for the sailor. For the soldier it was just the beginning. Naval Overseas Transport Service operated 490 vessels between American ports and base ports in France.

BUILDING A THOUSAND SHIPS

Every soldier carried to France required the transportation of 5 tons of food supplies and munitions a year. To fill the demand for tonnage, American shipyards built hundreds of cargo ships. Note ship nearing completion.

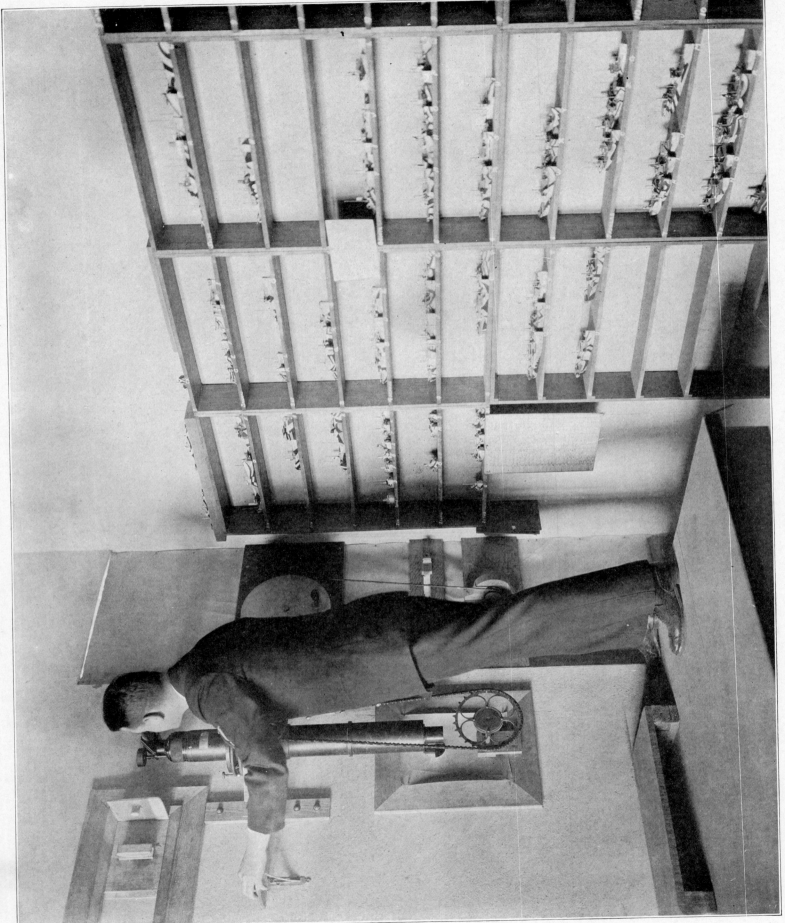

FOOLING FRITZ

The important work of camouflaging American ships was assigned to men who were experts in the scientific laws of refraction of light, color values, high and low visibility and many other details. This man is studying the effect of a camouflage pattern through a periscope.

"WE ARE READY NOW, SIR"

These words of Lieut. Commander J. K. Taussig upon the arrival of the first U. S. destroyers to join the British fleet were typical of the attitude of the whole navy. The U. S. S. Trippe is proof that what he said was true.

A BULL-DOG IN LEASH

Here the U. S. S. Stevens shows a different type of camouflage than that in the view above. It was not the purpose of camouflage to make the ship invisible, but to deceive the observer as to its size, shape and course.

NOW YOU SEE THEM, NOW YOU DON'T

Among these designers of navy camouflage are some American artists who did their bit by creating effective dazzle patterns. The effect was carefully tested on models before being used on warships and transports. It is impossible to estimate how many ships were saved by this work.

BAD NEWS FOR SUBMARINES

This array of American sea power includes U. S. Cruiser Melville, and part of a squadron of destroyers. Eighty-five American destroyers and three Russian destroyers, manned by American crews, were on duty in European waters.

THE BEGINNING OF THE END

The first convoy to arrive in France. Sailing in a dense fog on June 14, 1917, the ships docked at St. Nazaire on June 26. German submarines attacked the convoy at 10:15 P.M. on June 22 but not a ship nor a man was injured.

THE ANSWER TO THE SUBMARINE

America's ship building program during the war was the most stupendous ever undertaken. The destroyer program alone called for 275 ships, costing more than the whole active navy when we entered the war. One destroyer, the Ward, was launched 17 days after its keel was laid.

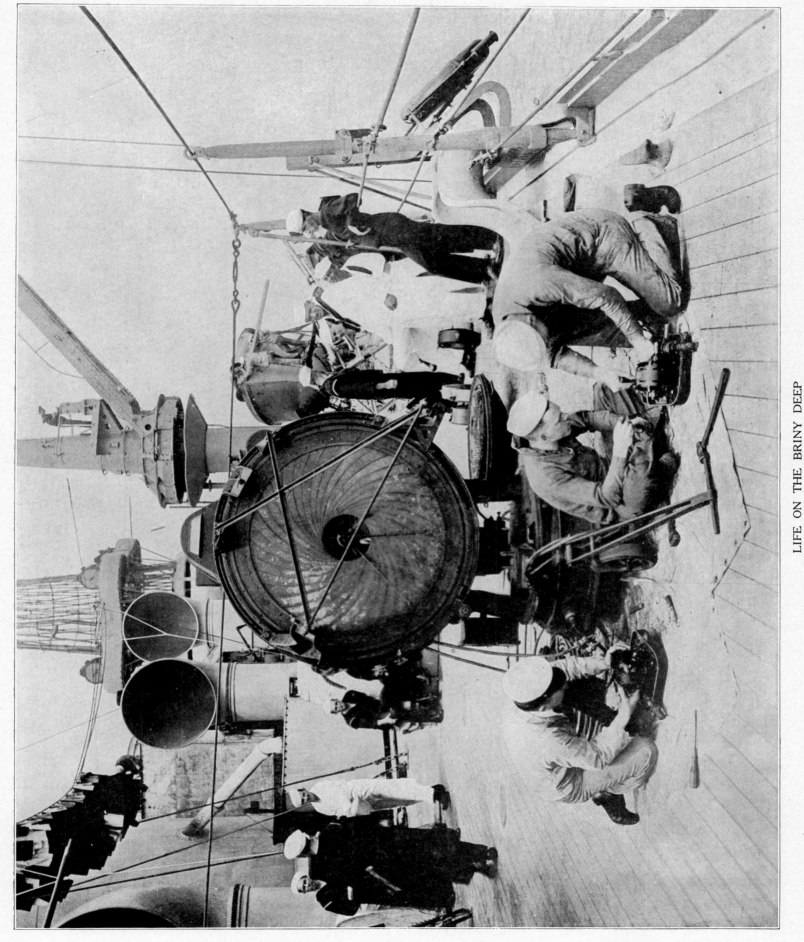

LIFE ON THE BRINY DEEP

Upon entry of the United States into the war, the navy immediately took over the patrolling of all American waters, relieving British warships for European service. It was vital that the route from England to Mexico be kept clear as the British navy was dependent on Mexican oil.

DOG EAT DOG

United States Submarine, AL-9, off the coast of Ireland. Cruising submarines remained submerged during the day, reconnoitering with periscopes every 15 minutes. At night they rose to take in air and recharge their batteries.

A DOSE OF THEIR OWN MEDICINE

Loading torpedoes on an American submarine at Bantry Bay. Captured German officers stated that they got used to depth charges but lived in constant dread of submarines. They never knew when an enemy torpedo might hit them.

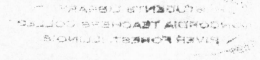

206

GLAD TO BE ALIVE

While on duty the AL-10 was once mistaken for a U-Boat and attacked by a U. S. destroyer. Unable to identify itself, the submarine dived but was bombed with depth charges. It emerged again and was finally recognized.

"CINDERELLAS OF THE FLEET"

Over 400 of these sub-chasers were built during the war. Manned mostly by American college men, they were intended primarily to guard the home shores. Many were sent across where they served effectively against the submarines.

A HOSPITAL FOR WARSHIPS

Bow view of a United States ship in a floating dry dock. This mammoth device made it possible to get at the bottom of the largest battleship for overhauling or repairs in short order and without the necessity of a long trip to a permanent base thousands of miles across the water.

MUTE TESTIMONY

Only a circle of oil on the surface of the water marks the spot where the dreaded German submarine U-42 was sunk. A diver is about to descend in search of further evidence. During the war, 205 German and 8 Austrian submarines, with their crews, went to Davy Jones' locker.

TO SHUT THE HORNETS IN THEIR NESTS

Taking mines aboard the U. S. S. San Francisco. Mines were planted by running them down rails which extended over the stern. This ship would plant a mine every 11½ seconds over a period of more than two hours.

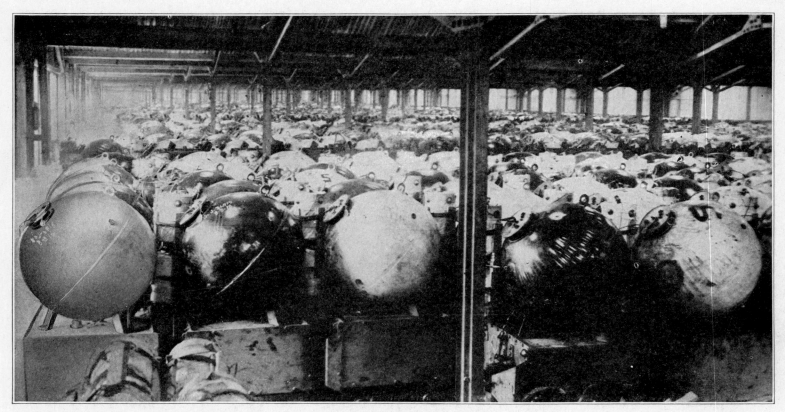

AMERICA BUILT 100,000 MINES

A mine depot at Inverness, Scotland. American inventors developed an electrical firing apparatus which exploded the mine if a submarine passed close to it. The explosion would occur even though there were no direct contact.

SOWING SEEDS OF DESTRUCTION

American mine laying fleet in the North Sea. The ships shown are the Canonicus, Canandaigua, Aroostook, Quine-bang, Saranac, Roanoke, Housatonic and Baltimore. In the North Sea Mine Barrage, Americans laid 56,611 mines.

DEATH FROM THE DEPTHS

A mine exploding. The completion of the North Sea Mine Barrage was devastating to the morale of German submarine crews, resulting in a mutiny of the crews and the abandonment of the submarine campaign on Oct. 26, 1918.

THE FERRY TO FRANCE

One of the most thrilling sights of the war—a convoy of transports approaching the shores of France. Not one American soldier, aboard a troop transport manned by the United States Navy, lost his life through enemy action.

BATTLE WAGON

The monster guns of the U. S. S. Pennsylvania. Five American battleships joined the British Grand Fleet. The rest of the fleet, including the Pennsylvania, remained to keep open the lanes between America and Europe.

SPURLOS VERSENKT

U. S. Transport, Covington, just after being torpedoed while returning from France. "The bugle sounded 'Silence' and the men went down the Jacob's ladders as if at drill." The crew was rescued by the destroyer, Smith.

ABANDON SHIP

Photograph of the escape of the passengers from the sinking ship, Sonay. The small black dots bobbing up and down are passengers swimming around in the sea. The ship sank within four minutes after being torpedoed.

ON GUARD

American destroyers on their way to meet a convoy. From 300 to 500 miles from land, at some spot on the vast ocean, punctual to the minute, these destroyers will pick up the convoy to escort it through the submarine danger zone. The picture was taken from the U. S. S. Stockton.

FERRETS OF THE SEA

Equipped with delicate under-water listening devices, submarine chasers, operating in groups of three, located submarines by triangulating the sound of submarine motors. They then dashed over the spot dropping depth bombs.

THESE CAME OUT ALIVE

German U-58 surrendering to U. S. S. Fanning. When Lieut. Com. Carpenter accepted the surrender, a German sailor opened the sea cocks and scuttled the ship. The crew jumped into the water and was rescued, losing one man.

BLINDING THE ENEMY

Smoke screen as laid by American destroyers. Although used in many ways, the smoke screen was particularly helpful when a ship had been disabled. Hiding the injured vessel from the enemy, it protected it from further attack during repairs or while the ship was helped into port.

THE ANSWER TO BIG BERTHA

Five 14-inch naval guns, constructed by the Baldwin Locomotive Works and under command of Rear-Admiral C. P. Plunkett, U. S. N., were in action in France. They were used to silence "Big Bertha," the German super-gun and to destroy railroad yards at Laon, Montmedy and Conflans.

THE ARMY, TOO, HAD RAILWAY GUNS

An 8-inch narrow gauge train of the Coast Artillery Corps. The C. A. C. usually remains at home to guard coast and harbor entrances. With the German navy bottled up at Kiel, several units were released for duty overseas.

THE SCOURGE OF GERMAN RAILWAYS

The railroad from Metz to Sedan ran parallel to the front lines, enabling the Germans to rush troops to any threatened point. By destroying yards and switches, these naval guns aided in hastening the end of the war.

OFF TO STRAFE THE GERMANS

The excellent French roads, when undamaged by artillery fire, made it possible to move long range guns rapidly. This U. S. Coast Artillery gun is enroute to a new post to continue its work of disrupting enemy communications.

FOUR OUT OF FOUR

This 340 mm. of the U. S. Coast Artillery fired four shots into German lines, Oct. 12, 1918. Airplane observers reported each one a direct hit. Railway yards, bridgeheads, enemy headquarters—were targets for these guns.

DIRECT HIT

Sometimes Germans made direct hits too. A high-powered "Filloux 155" and tractor of the Coast Artillery knocked 40 ft., overturned and the muzzle buried in the road by a direct hit near Charpentry, Oct. 5, 1918. 2nd Lt. J. F. Lewis, Battery F, 56th C. A. C., examining breach.

BRINGING FOOD FOR GUNS

Each one of the naval guns used in France required a train of 15 cars for its maintenance. In addition to ammunition cars like those shown here, they required workshop cars, a crane car, berth, kitchen and headquarters cars.

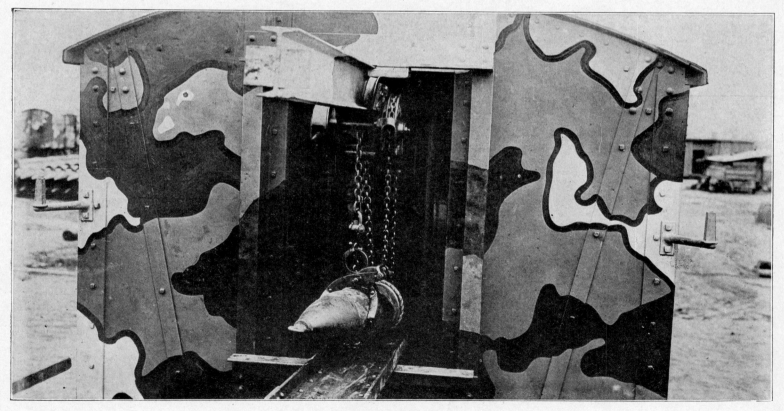

YANKEE INGENUITY

Shells for the largest long range guns weighed 1400 pounds. By adapting machinery used in manufacturing plants at home for use in ammunition cars, these shells could be handled quickly and easily. Note use of camouflage.

IN SUNNY ITALY

To strengthen the morale of the Italians and to weaken that of the Austrians, the 332nd Inf., 83rd Div., was sent to operate with the Italian Armies. Upon capture of Fiume, former Austrian submarine base, the "Ferencz Ferdinand" became the headquarters of American troops in Italy.

AGAINST THE PASSAGE OF THE PIAVE

Just as American troops in France helped the Allies stem the German tide at the Marne, so the Americans in Italy aided the Italians in repulsing the Austrians at the Piave River. Member of the 332nd Inf. firing from a trench.

BOMBING THE AUSTRIAN LINES

332nd. Inf., 83rd Div., lobbing hand grenades in Austrian positions near 2nd Bn. headquarters, near Varago, Italy, Sept. 16, 1918. Troops of leading Allied nations operated on Italian front as well as western front in France.

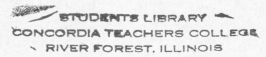
223

AUSTRIA BOWS

This picture shows the triumphal entry of the 332nd Infantry into Cormons, the first town of any size in Austria to be occupied by American troops, on November 13, 1918. The Austrian Armistice was signed Nov. 3, 1918, eight days before the signing of the armistice with Germany.

HALLOWED QUIETS OF THE PAST

An American sailor and American and Italian soldiers in the courtyard of the ancient Tersato Castle, Fiume, Italy. First used by the Austrians as a naval base for their operations in the Adriatic, Fiume later became the headquarters of the United States forces in Italy.

PRESSING THE AUSTRIAN RETREAT

American patrols, close to the retreating Austrians, resting at Codroipo, Italy, shortly after driving out the enemy. After the last Austrian drive at the Piave River, June, 1918, the Allies steadily drove the Austrians back.

UNDER SOUTHERN SKIES

A platoon of the 332nd Infantry, 83rd Division, marching along the Royal Dyke in Italy. The picture shows the third line of trenches in this sector to be held by the American forces during the battle of the Piave River.

THE RED CROSS TO THE FRONT

Even before American combat troops arrived on the Italian front, a number of ambulance companies were sent there because of a shortage of this type of equipment among the Italians. This ambulance section arrived in June, 1917.

UPON THE PLEASANT RIVER

Because of difference in terrain, military operations in Italy differed from those on the Western Front. 3rd Battalion, 332nd Inf., crossing a river in pontoons directed by Italian veterans, Porto di Fiera, Italy, Oct. 6, 1918.

TO THE LAND OF THE MUSCOVITES

American troops landing at Vladivostok, Siberia. Attempting to overcome the blow suffered through the Russian Revolution and Bolshevik surrender to Germany, the Allies sent troops to assist White Russian forces against the Reds.

LUMBER FOR DOUGHBOYS' HOMES

Upon the arrival of American forces in Russia, it was necessary to construct barracks capable of withstanding the rigors of a winter near the Arctic Circle. Many women were engaged in this work but at half the pay of the men.

SUPPLIES FOR THE SIX MONTHS' NIGHT

Navigation at Archangel, Russia, base for North Russian Expeditionary Forces, was open only a few months each year. It was necessary to concentrate great quantities of supplies to carry the troops through the long Arctic winter.

AMONG THE FIRST ARRIVALS

This was one of the first United States official pictures from the American front in Russia. It shows the unloading of American ambulances for the use of the North Russian Expeditionary Forces—the first of these to arrive.

"'NEATH THE LIGHT OF THE PALE NORTHERN STAR"

An airplane view of Archangel, headquarters of the American Expeditionary Forces in Russia. This force consisted principally of units of the 85th Division. From there, the army worked south along the Archangel-Vologda Railroad.

OH, FOR THE LIFE OF A SAILOR

Sailors from U. S. S. Olympia formed a landing force under Lt. Hicks and participated in driving the Bolsheviki out of Archangel. In conjunction with army troops, they pursued the Reds during 4 weeks of continuous fighting.

A RACE WITH ARCTIC ICE

To reach Archangel, ships had to go 350 miles north of the Arctic Circle. Navigation was open only a few months. The steamer Seattle is rushing to unload her cargo, on Oct. 21, 1918, before the ice blocks her passage home.

THE HOME OF AMERICANS IN RUSSIA

The olive drab (O. D.) of the United States Army soon became a familiar sight in Archangel's principal streets. In the background is seen the city's famous cathedral, the domes and spires of which glitter with gold leaf.

CHILL WINDS WHISTLE SHRILL

Bolshevik prisoners of war in Archangel, guarded by American sentries, digging pieces of lumber out of the snow for use in camp construction. They are probably Red sailors from Russian destroyers taken over by the Allies and operated in the White Sea by Americans and White Russians.

CAMP MICHIGAN

American Army engineers rushing to finish one of the barracks of the camp of the Expeditionary Forces in Archangel. This camp was like a little American frontier city. The construction of buildings during the autumn of 1918 was a race with the weather that was won just in time.

BREAD WHICH STRENGTHENS MAN'S HEART

A detail from the 2nd Bn., 339th Inf., 85th Div., unloading supplies at a warehouse in Archangel where all Allied stores were held. The uniforms are not what doughboys wore in France, but are more comfortable in a Russian winter.

COUNTING NOSES

Former soldiers of the Czar who turned Bolshevik and were later captured by the Americans along the Vologda Railway. The prisoners were brought to Archangel by sailors and are being turned over to the army for safe keeping.

WHEN WINTER COMES

Except for the barbed wire entanglements in the foreground, this picture, showing the American front in Russia, might be mistaken for one of an early period in America—a clearing in the woods; in the center, a log blockhouse.

RATION DETAIL

The picture shows Allied troops drawing rations from a train on the Vologda railway in North Russia. A Poilu is at the head of the queue receiving a quarter of beef; next in line are two Yanks, then a Russ, and two Tommies.

235

GUARDING LINES OF COMMUNICATIONS

A blockhouse built by men from Michigan and Wisconsin of Company I, 339th Infantry, 85th Division, to guard a railroad yard in North Russia. The blockhouse was necessary not only as a protection for soldiers from enemy attacks, but also to shelter them from the severe winter weather.

THIS IS THE FOREST PRIMEVAL

Unlike the Western Front, military operations in North Russia were almost entirely of the open variety. Advancing in small detachments, Americans pursued the Bolsheviki in much the same way their forefathers fought the Indians. American infantryman on outpost duty south of Archangel.

A ROUGH WEARY ROAD

After picking their way, for seventeen hours, through mud and swamp in a vain attempt to flank a force of Bolsheviki, these doughboys of the American Expeditionary Forces in Russia pause at the edge of a forest to dry their home-knit socks at a camp fire and snatch a bite to eat.

SNOW SHALL BE THEIR WINDING SHEET

Final rites. Taps being blown at the grave of an American soldier of the 85th Division who was killed during an attack on the Bolshevik forces in North Russia in October, 1918. The bodies of some of those who died in Russia were returned to the United States in 1934.